GENERATIONS

at

SCHOOL

This book is dedicated to two educators who have profoundly influenced the professional lives of school leaders—Roland Barth and Rick DuFour. We are forever grateful for their wisdom, passion, and inspiration.

GENERATIONS
—at—
SCHOOL

Building an Age-Friendly Learning Community

Suzette Lovely
Austin G. Buffum

Foreword by Roland S. Barth

CORWIN PRESS
A SAGE Publications Company
Thousand Oaks, CA 91320

For information:

Corwin Press
A Sage Publications Company
2455 Teller Road
Thousand Oaks, California 91320
www.corwinpress.com

Sage Publications Ltd.
1 Oliver's Yard
55 City Road
London EC1Y 1SP
United Kingdom

Sage Publications India Pvt. Ltd.
B-42, Panchsheel Enclave
Post Box 4109
New Delhi 110 017 India

Sage Publications Asia-Pacific Pvt. Ltd
33 Pekin Street #02-01
Far East Square
Singapore 048763

Printed in the United States of America

Library of Congress Cataloging-in-Publication Data

Lovely, Suzette, 1958-
Generations at school: Building an age-friendly learning community/Suzette Lovely & Austin G. Buffum.
    p. cm.
Includes bibliographical references and index.
ISBN-13: 978–1-4129–2727–7 (cloth: alk. paper)
ISBN-13: 978–1-4129–2728–4 (pbk.: alk. paper)
    1. School personnel management—United States. 2. Intergenerational relations—United States. 3. Intergenerational communication—United States.
4. Teacher-administrator relationships—United States. I. Buffum, Austin G. II. Title.
LB2831.5.L68 2007

07 08 09 10 11 10 9 8 7 6 5 4 3 2 1

Acquisitions Editor:	Elizabeth Brenkus
Editorial Assistant:	Desirée Enayati
Production Editor:	Beth A. Bernstein
Copy Editor:	Brenda Weight
Typesetter:	C&M Digitals (P) Ltd.
Proofreader:	Theresa Kay
Indexer:	Rick Hurd
Cover Designer:	Audrey Snodgrass
Graphic Designer:	Karine Hovsepian

Contents

Foreword

Samuel Johnson is reported to have once observed, "that which is written without pleasure shall be read without pleasure." (As one who has read his share of doctoral dissertations, I can attest to the veracity of his words!) But the converse is also true: That which is written *with* pleasure shall be read with pleasure.

The little volume you are about to read was clearly written with a great deal of pleasure. And I am confident that you will find pleasure in reading it. I have!

For me, the pleasure comes from the authors' identification and analysis of a phenomenon in our schools of which I have been largely unaware: that the adults who staff our schools—teachers, principals, guidance counselors, librarians, custodians—come from four distinct generations, each of which represents a dramatically different culture. And I had been unaware of how desperately this topic needs to become a "discussable" in our schools.

We educators are all too aware of the many divides that characterize (and often imperil) our schools: teacher and administrator, adult and child, male and female, black and white, smart and not as smart. Well, the divides among our colleagues, the Veterans (born 1922–1943), the Baby Boomers (born 1944–1960), Generation X (born 1960–1980), and the Millennials (born 1980–2000), are every bit as consequential, if not as apparent.

The characteristics and idiosyncrasies that members of each of these generations bring into the schoolhouse have an extraordinary influence on the day-to-day life of the school and on its culture.

Unfortunately, too often these influences are damaging to our relationships with one another and to the important work we aspire to do of educating youngsters.

While we cannot change these givens, while we cannot mandate harmony, uniformity, and collegiality, we *can* understand them. And understanding them is the first step in transforming these differences from a curse into a blessing.

The gift of the book you are about to encounter is that it helps us understand our multigenerational workforce. And equally valuable, it offers very specific and helpful tips for addressing what the authors call our "employee stew" (e.g., school leaders can play up the role of the Veteran as "honored historian by emphasizing the need to take newcomers under their wing and share their wisdom").

Each generation can benefit from the different perspectives and strengths of the others. So just as the multiaged classroom offers many advantages in promoting students' learning, so can the multiaged schoolhouse offer advantages in building a professional learning community.

It's been said that the true act of discovery lies not in seeing new lands but in seeing with new eyes. You, dear reader, are in store for a major discovery!

—Roland S. Barth

Preface

The Demographic Divide

The composition of the workplace—whether people are young or old, black or white, conservative or liberal, urbanite or country folk— shapes every aspect of an organization's being. Complicating matters is the fact that the workforce is changing drastically as Americans live longer, more immigrants find jobs, and older employees postpone retirement. For a school, the plurality of those who serve students controls its destiny. School systems cannot contemplate their future without understanding the demographic DNA of the staff, parents, and students entwined within it.

SIZING UP THE POPULATION

To get a glimpse of what lies ahead for public education, let's size up our population using the structure of a pyramid. In most countries, the babies and young people at the base surpass the shrinking pool of elders at the top. Currently, however, the population pyramid in the United States has a bulging midsection of Baby Boomers who are aging slowly while steadfastly retaining their powerful place in the workforce.

According to demographers, the pudgy pyramid is going to trim down in the next decade and take on the shape of an hourglass (Zolli, 2006). With semiretired Boomers on top and Millennials (who are predicted to surpass the Baby Boom generation in size) at the bottom, Generation X will find itself squeezed into the middle. As imagined, the hourglass society working and weighing in on the educational issues will have a dramatic impact on what happens in schools.

Most educators aren't fully prepared for this transformation, nor do they understand the generational lines in the sand that may be drawn during such rapidly changing times. Adding to the dilemma is the reality that the generational blueprint of a school staff is seldom touched on in the training of future administrators nor is it being addressed in leadership development for current superintendents or principals. With the professional learning community movement pushing for more collaboration in the schoolhouse, it will be hard to mind the gap without looking at the cross-age differences involved.

WHO'S SIMMERING IN YOUR STEW?

This book is designed to introduce school leaders to the traits, hot buttons, and tipping points of four distinct generations working in American schools today: Veterans (born 1922–1943), Baby Boomers (born 1944–1960), Generation X (born 1960–1980), and Millennials (born 1980–2000). Included in each chapter are specific ideas and tools to help readers not only understand and manage the mix but also successfully foster coalescence among intergenerational teams.

While it is important to be familiar with the many ingredients simmering in your employee stew, it is not enough to stop there. It is also necessary to respond to the generational appetite of the customers who sample the daily cuisine. To that end, we have devoted an entire chapter to describing the Millennial students sitting in our classroom seats. And an additional chapter is included to assist readers in dealing with Millennials' parents who constantly hover and dote upon them. Clearly, the demographic milieu is no longer a singular sensation with similar occupational ideals, educational values, and outlook on life.

FIXING FLAWS, FLAWED FIXES

Throughout our nation's history, each generation has been educated to fix the flaws that surfaced during the previous generation's youth (Howe & Strauss, 2000). In fact, the one thing we can count on with an age-driven society is that it will be the distinct opposite of the one that came before it. The premise behind zero tolerance affirms this phenomenon quite well.

Since the 1990s, crusaders from all sides of the political spectrum have convinced the public that unless bad kids are removed from school, teachers can't teach and students can't learn. As a result, Millennials are the recipients of the most severe discipline ever imposed upon children.

The irony is that such harsh measures have been adopted to cope with the mess rebellious Boomer and Generation X parents actually created. Needless to say, Millennials are the most compliant, achievement-oriented schoolhouse occupants in years.

The push to bring technology to every campus in the nation is another illustration of this hopscotch pattern. In the 1980s, principals scurried to get schools up to speed by purchasing Commodore computers for each classroom and setting up Apple IIe labs. Despite having access to these newfangled machines, most Veteran and Baby Boomer faculty stuck with their trusty 8 mm films and overhead projectors. With no relevant training on how to use the technology, predominant thinking was that students merely had to learn about computers, not necessarily learn from them or with them.

Meanwhile, the first batch of Millennials began arriving in classrooms in the late 1980s. They had learned how to manipulate a mouse before holding their own bottle. From Game Boys, to fiber-optic friendships, to twitch speed, students went global while teachers were still figuring out how to program the VCR. Computers are as familiar to a Millennial as a television is to a Baby Boomer.

PRIORITIES HAVE CHANGED

Under a prevailing belief that young people are getting older younger, school-age children expect to have a say in everything, including how they are educated. A teen in one recent study chortled, "People have to realize that *we* will set the standards and *we* will raise the bar" (Geraci, 2005).

For teachers, presenting the same material in the same fashion in which they may have learned it can lead to a cycle of boredom, especially as schools face such stiff competition for students' attention. Home school, charter school, and virtual school movements are gaining momentum as parents strive to ensure their talented kids are taught what they need to know in the manner Mom and Dad see fit.

Stepping outside our generational comfort zone is vital if we as teachers, principals, superintendents, central office leaders, and policymakers hope to reach this more tenacious clientele. Monumental issues such as poverty, global warming, and foreign competition require adolescents to leave high school with a bank of knowledge no other generation has needed before. This book will help readers build understanding around the multiage impressions that engulf their own workplace. As new ways to leverage every asset are discovered, the universal goal of improving learning for all students is accomplished.

Is it possible to turn our schools into Romper Room, where people work and play splendidly together? Absolutely! Promoting an age-friendly workplace is easy if leaders set egos aside and avoid being judgmental. Paying attention to the generational trademarks of stakeholders is a sensible way to bridge the divide and spawn the collective responsibility necessary to get the results educators want, taxpayers expect, and students deserve.

Acknowledgments

Corwin Press gratefully acknowledges the contributions of the following reviewers:

Christi Buell
Principal
Neihardt Elementary
Millard Public Schools
Omaha, NE

Mary Lynne Derrington
Superintendent
Blaine School District
Blaine, WA

Gerard A. Dery
Director, Zone 1, National
    Association of Elementary
    School Principals
Principal, Nessacus Regional
    Middle School
Dalton, MA

Laurie Emery
Principal
Old Vail Middle School
Vail, AZ

Mary Beth Genovese-Scullion
Director of Instruction,
    Assessment, & Staff
    Development
Lockport, NY

Douglas Gordon Hesbol
Superintendent
Laraway CCSD #70C
Joliet, IL

Jean Kueker
Retired Professor & Adjunct
    Instructor
Our Lady of the Lake University
San Antonio, TX

Jennifer Williams
Adjunct Professor
Boise State University
2002 Idaho Teacher of the Year
Boise, ID

About the Authors

 **Suzette Lovely** is the Deputy Superintendent, Personnel Services, in the Capistrano Unified School District in Orange County, California. She has spent 24 years in public education as a teacher, assistant principal, elementary principal, and director of elementary operations. She also serves as an adjunct faculty member at Chapman University teaching courses in educational administration.

Lovely has authored two previous books: *Setting Leadership Priorities: What's Necessary, What's Nice and What's Got to Go* (Corwin Press, 2006) and *Staffing the Principalship: Finding, Coaching and Mentoring School Leaders* (ASCD, 2004). She is also a staff writer for the Master Teacher publications.

The author resides in San Clemente, California, and can be contacted through the Capistrano Unified School District at 33122 Valle Road, San Juan Capistrano, CA, 92675, or via e-mail at slovely@capousd.org or sue .lovely@cox.net.

 **Austin G. Buffum,** EdD, recently retired as the senior deputy superintendent of the Capistrano Unified School District, serving over 50,000 students in South Orange County, California. During his 34-year career in public education, he has been a music teacher and coordinator, elementary school principal, curriculum director, and assistant superintendent. Dr. Buffum was selected as the 2006 Curriculum and Instruction Administrator of the Year by the Association of California School Administrators.

Dr. Buffum attended the Principals' Center at the Harvard Graduate School of Education in 1991, and continues to admire and build upon the work of its founder, Roland Barth. Following that experience, Dr. Buffum led the Capistrano Unified School District's K–12 instructional program on an increasingly collaborative path toward operating as a professional learning community. Dr. Buffum has presented at scores of regional and national conferences and currently serves as Adjunct Professor of Educational Leadership at Chapman University and California State University, Fullerton, in Orange County. He is in demand as an educational consultant, speaking to schools, districts, and departments of education across the nation about his passion for professional learning communities on behalf of Solution Tree, Inc. Dr. Buffum can be reached via e-mail at abuffum@pacbell.net.

The Generations at Work in Schools

Every few hundred years in Western history . . . we cross a "divide."
Within a few short years, society rearranges itself—its worldview,
its basic values, its social and political structure, its arts, its key
institutions.

—Peter Drucker

From bowties and brooches to tank tops and tattoos, the canvas of the modern schoolhouse is changing. And it's not just students who look and act differently nowadays. Teachers, administrators, and parents are morphing too. Enter a campus and you might find faculty members showing off their latest nose piercings, while their ponytailed principal cruises the corridors in his Dockers and polo shirt. As older employees huddle in the staff lounge lamenting about how "things ain't what they used to be," the twenty-something parent volunteer making copies in the workroom hardly bats an eye.

According to the bestselling book *Generations at Work* (Zemke, Raines, & Filipczak, 2000), the American workforce has never been so diverse, yet so uniquely singular. No other country in the world can boast such a rich blend of race, gender, ethnicity, and age in its workplace. One of the most significant, and potentially problematic, effects of such diversity is the growing generational infusion that brings old, young, and in-betweens together in the same employment venue. Whether by choice or necessity, senior teachers are postponing retirement while those graduating from college are launching their careers. For school systems, a multigenerational workforce can be both a blessing and a curse.

THE PERFECT STORM

As the end of the twentieth century drew near, teachers and administrators found themselves whirling inside the vortex of shifting ideology. Between 1992 and 1999, the educational community was tossed around from autonomy to accountability, from restructuring to reform, from socialization to standards, from teaching to testing, from menus to mandates, and from *every child happy* to *every child a reader.* No wonder educators cruised into the millennium feeling a bit dizzy.

Confusion in California, for example, puts the dilemma into perspective. In July 1996 the state legislature poured $771 million into schools to lower class size in grades K–3 (CSR Research Consortium, 2002). This massive reform was tied to ten reading initiatives and 22 other programs all launched around the same time. Elementary teachers quickly became overwhelmed. Depending on their generational rank, these schoolhouse sailors either (a) decided "this too shall pass" and stayed below deck, (b) spent 12 hours a day in the eye of the storm trying to batten down their curriculum, or (c) jumped ship.

Although there is general consensus among the educational community that the shift from teaching to learning is a good thing, theories abound as to the best way to tackle such a lofty endeavor. Without looking more closely at the cross-age profile inside schools, it may be difficult to achieve and sustain coalescence—especially during the stormy seas ahead. Bridging the gap and managing the friction means employee wants, needs, hopes, and fears have to be noticed and appreciated.

WHO'S WHO? A SNAPSHOT OF FOUR LIVING GENERATIONS

Table 1.1   Who's Who? A Snapshot of Four Living Generations

Generation/Age Span	General Characteristics	Defining Moments/Cultural Icons
Veterans (born 1922–1943) 38 million Americans	Formed worldview during hard times of Depression and WWII Built much of the nation's infrastructure Believe in duty before pleasure Spend conservatively Embrace values that speak to family, home, patriotism	The Great Depression Bombing of Pearl Harbor The Golden Era of Radio Superman FDR, Patton, Eisenhower

Generation/Age Span	General Characteristics	Defining Moments/Cultural Icons
Baby Boomers (born 1944–1960) 64 million Americans	Grew up in optimistic times of economic expansion Think of themselves as "cool" and "stars of the show" Covet status and power; driven to succeed Are service oriented Tend to be competitive because of their group size · Pursue own gratification, often at a price to themselves and their families	Vietnam War Assassinations Civil rights movement Women's lib The peace sign *Captain Kangaroo* The Beatles
Generation X (born 1960–1980) 39 million Americans	Raised in an era of soaring divorce rates, struggling economy, and fallen heroes Are self-reliant and skeptical of authority Seek sense of family through network of friends and work relationships Maintain nontraditional orientation of time and space Eschew being labeled in any way, shape, or form	Microwaves, computer games, VCRs Nixon resignation MTV AIDS Extreme sports *The Simpsons*
Millennials (born 1980–2000) 79 million Americans	Feel wanted and indulged by parents Lead busy, overplanned lives Embrace core values similar to Veterans—optimism, civic duty, confidence, morality Are well mannered and polite Able to use technology in unforeseen ways	9-11 Columbine The Internet X Games Reality TV The Olson twins

SOURCE: Adapted from U.S. Census Bureau, 2004; Zemke, Raines, & Filipczak, 2000.

The current public school workforce comprises four distinct groups: Veterans, Baby Boomers, Generation X, and Millennials. Although there are no hard-and-fast rules about where one generation ends and another begins, demographers such as Neil Howe and William Strauss, who have studied generations dating back to the colonial period, note that specific life events tie a group together through shared experiences, hardships, social norms, and turning points. These common threads create self-sustaining links that cause people of a given era to maintain similar attitudes, ambitions, and synergy. Consider the profile of Veteran superintendents as a case in point. In their minds, age correlates with rank and status in the organization. Employees move up the ladder one rung at a time through perseverance, loyalty, and hard work. Older leaders tend to be formal, steeped in tradition, and have difficulty with change or ambiguity.

Generation X, on the other hand, came of age in times of corporate downsizing, a struggling economy, and an explosion of technology that allowed work to be done differently. Self-reliance, an impatience for bureaucracy, and the ability to change directions on a dime can make them seem irreverent to a Veteran. Generation X is not interested in working around the clock or keeping score of who has paid their dues. While a Veteran might ask, "How did he become a superintendent at age 35? He's just a boy!" the thirty-something superintendent is likely to respond, "Send me an e-mail if you have a concern. And, take a little time off if the pressure is getting to you."

Today's living generations span roughly 80 years. People born within the same general timeframe—about every 18 to 25 years—are referred to as a *cohort* (Zemke, Raines, & Filipczak, 2000). Key life experiences from entering school, reaching puberty, graduating from high school, starting work, getting married, and having children define the core beliefs among each cohort. Although every human being has his or her own unique personality, many people underestimate how similar they are to their generational counterparts. Despite one's race, gender, socioeconomic status, and moral or religious views, the music, politics, heroes, headlines, scandals, and world events shared by an age group cannot be weaned from one's system. No matter how different individuals may be in mind, body, or spirit, they are age-bound in perceptions, passions, and pleasures. Common exposure breeds common thoughts.

To get a glimpse of who's who, let's examine the generational landscape of today's workplace:

Veterans (born before 1943): Described by Tom Brokaw as "the greatest generation," this cohort won a world war, rebuilt the nation's economy after a debilitating Depression, sent a man to the moon, and coined the phrase *American values*. Veterans come from a mold of honor and dedication. If they commit to something, you can take their word to the bank.

Throughout their formative years, Veterans had to make do or go without. After decades of frugality, they've amassed a whopping 75 percent of the financial assets in the United States (Zemke, Raines, & Filipczak, 2000). Despite entering their golden years with money to burn, Matures—as they are sometimes called—think nothing of driving across town to save ten cents on a gallon of gasoline. If you remember VJ Day, you are probably a Veteran.

Largely responsible for creating the infrastructure of American schools, Veterans are convinced that students need to be taught in a disciplined, orderly, and standardized fashion. To them, the hierarchical nature of the military and manufacturing—with a strong leader in charge—made perfectly good sense in schools too. Careful spending is another Veteran trademark. If you don't believe it, check out the supply cabinet of your oldest teacher or peruse the end-of-year carryover of your most senior principal. After all, one never knows when eight staplers or thousands of unencumbered dollars might come in handy.

Baby Boomers (born 1944 to 1960): The post–WWII baby boom era marked a reversal in the declining population trend that had stymied American growth for decades. Baby Boomers were the first generation in which child rearing was considered a pleasure rather than an economic or biological reality. Not only were these babies wanted, Dr. Spock implored parents to love and cherish them. His book instructed adults to go light on punishment and heavy on reason, with the main objective to make children happy.

Such overindulgence likely explains Baby Boomer patterns of excess, self-absorption, and insistence on getting their way. As trendsetters, Baby Boomers have made turning 50 fashionable and transformed fitness, spirituality, and cosmetic surgery into billion dollar industries. From Bill Clinton, to Martha Stewart, to Madonna, their ability to reinvent themselves is legendary.

Because there were so many of them, Baby Boomers were the first group of school-aged children to be graded on cooperation and "shares materials with classmates" (Raines, 1997, p. 27). Hence, teamwork is in their blood. They also grew up being told, "Ask not what your country can do for you, but instead what you can do for your country." As a result, these overachievers devised the 60-hour workweek with the hope that a better life was just around the corner. Those who recall the day President Kennedy was shot are likely to be members of the Baby Boom generation.

Many school systems are managed by Baby Boomer principals and superintendents, which helps to explain why reforms and innovations never cease. This is the cohort that has a hard time saying no and can't quite grasp the concept that less is more. Baby Boomers remain the dominant force in education today, first, because of their sheer size and second, because they are not all that anxious to retire. Their influence over what happens in schools is expected to continue for several more years.

Generation X (born 1960 to 1980): Sometimes thought of as detached, morose, and unmotivated, Generation X has had a tough go of things. Conceived in the shadow of the Baby Boomers, this smaller cohort has struggled to compete. Consequently, their psyche is shaped by a survivor mentality. They survived the divorce of their parents. They survived joint custody and life as latchkey kids. They survived college on student loans and Top Ramen. They survived oil embargos, real estate plunges, and stock market crashes. And they continue to survive the roller coaster ride of dot.com meltdowns and outsourcing.

While the parents and grandparents of Generation X stuck with the same employer for most of their career, the average tenure for today's 25- to 34-year-old is 2.9 years (Bureau of Labor Statistics, 2004, September 21). At this rate, an "Xer" could change jobs as many as ten times before retirement. Such overexposure to hard knocks puts their distrust of authority and disdain for bureaucracy into perspective. As a cohort, they have lower-than-average expectations of what work can offer and aren't motivated by rewards that require perseverance or longevity. If you watched the *Challenger* disaster on a classroom TV, odds are good you belong to Generation X—although you dislike being labeled or lumped in with any mainstream group whatsoever.

What Generation X lacks in loyalty, they more than make up for in technical savvy and talent. Left alone to hook up their Atari and manipulate the microwave, this is the ingenious generation of eBay founder Pierre Omidyar, Larry Page and Sergey Brin of Google fame, and Michael Dell of Dell Computers. Their nontraditional approach to solving problems is an asset, especially in places such as schools, where it took twenty years to move the overhead projector from the bowling alley into the classroom. Although they don't always buy into the teamwork manifesto of their Boomer bosses, they are able to work on teams if given the discretion to complete tasks, make decisions, and implement solutions their own way.

Millennials (born 1980 to 2000): Also referred to as Generation Y, Echo Boomers, and Nexters, Millennials are expected to surpass Baby Boomers in size and achievement. Unrivaled as a consumer group, they average $100 a week in disposable income and influence $50 billion in annual family purchases (Zemke, Raines, & Filipczak, 2000). In 1999, the *Wall Street Journal* reported that 11 percent of the nation's 12- to 17-year-olds owned their own stock (Howe & Strauss, 2000). With unbridled spending power, America's youth exude a level of sophistication and tenacity that is sure to set any workplace on fire.

Adults are often surprised to learn that Millennials tend to subscribe to a strict moral code in which abstinence and zero tolerance hold sway. Most American teens actually enjoy spending time with their family and have glommed on to many of the same civic values embraced by the Veteran generation. Children who have the Columbine shootings and the morning of September 11 firmly etched into their young memories are Millennials.

With unlimited technology connecting them to people and places around the globe, today's youth have done and seen more than their parents or grandparents did in an entire lifetime. Thought to be the most open-minded generation in modern history, Millennials embrace group dating, biracial friendships, and study-abroad programs with a nonchalance that makes them color blind.

As the oldest Millennials graduate from high school and complete college, they are blossoming at a time when jobs are fairly abundant. For twenty-somethings arriving in our classrooms as the newest teachers, principals should be ready to satisfy their craving for ongoing learning experiences, include them in decisions, and assign them to supportive teams.

As with any label or generalization, not all peer groups fit into the same box. Certainly, stereotypes can interfere with performance and cause resentment. Therefore, a commonsense approach is necessary when hiring, mentoring, directing, or evaluating employees based on their generational coding. Knowing the underpinnings that bind colleagues together or set them apart is beneficial in establishing collaborative teams, building capacity, and bringing out the best in people.

Table 1.2, "The Generational Footprint of a Workplace," depicts the manner in which the different age groups perform on the job, integrate into teams, and lead others. As the portrait of each cadre unfolds, school leaders can hone in on strengths, make weaknesses irrelevant, and foster greater appreciation for diversity. Without such awareness or sensitivity, it is impossible to cultivate professional learning communities that are results based and improvement driven.

Table 1.2   The Generational Footprint of a Workplace

Generation/ Age Span	How They Perform on the Job	How They Integrate on Teams	How They Lead Others
Veterans Age Span 63 and older	Driven by rules and order Strive to uphold culture and traditions Able to leave work at work Need more time for orientation Find technology intimidating	Are okay with the power of collective action, as long as a central leader is in charge Respect experience Want to know where they stand and what's expected of them Eager to conform to group roles	Value dedication and loyalty Equate age with status/power Impose top-down structures Make most decisions themselves Keep work and personal life separate View change as disruptive and undesirable
Baby Boomers Age Span 45 to 62	Have a strong need to prove themselves to others May manipulate rules to meet own needs	Enjoy and value teamwork Expect group to stick to the schedule and agenda	Shy away from conflict Tend to lead through consensus Generally apply a participatory

(Continued)

Table 1.2 (Continued)

Generation/ Age Span	How They Perform on the Job	How They Integrate on Teams	How They Lead Others
	Deferential to authority Focus on product outcomes Can become political animals if turf is threatened Work long hours	Willing to go the extra mile Good at building rapport and solving problems Embrace equity and equality Want credit and respect for accomplishments	approach, but may struggle with delegation and empathy Embrace leadership trends and personal development Expect people to put in their time Less flexible with change
Generation X Age Span 25 to 44	Strive for balance, freedom, and flexibility Strong dislike for corporate politics, fancy titles, or rigid structures Expect to have fun at work Prefer independence and minimal supervision Good at multitasking Value process over product	Like to work on teams with informal roles and freedom to complete tasks their own way Do well on projects calling for technical competence and creativity Work best with teammates of their own choosing Detest being taken advantage of Struggle to build rapport with other group members	Drawn to leadership for altruistic reasons— not power or prestige Casual and laid-back Try to create an environment that is functional and efficient May lack tact and diplomacy Able to create and support alternative workplace structures Willing to challenge higher-ups Adapt easily to change
Millennials Age Span 24 and younger	Anxious to fit in Respectful of authority, but unafraid to approach their boss with concerns Value continuing education Exceptional at multitasking Drawn to organizations with career ladders and standardized pay/benefits	Accepting of group diversity Determined to achieve team goals Respond well to mentoring Enjoy working with idealistic people Expect to be included in decisions Need a bit more supervision and structure than other groups	Open to new ideas Able to work with varying employee styles and needs Prefer flattened hierarchy Hopeful and resilient Display more decorum and professionalism than Xers Lack experience handling conflict and difficult people

SOURCE: Adapted from Lancaster & Stillman, 2002; Raines, 2003; Zemke, Raines, & Filipczak, 2000.

ROAD MAPS AND ASPIRATIONS

Although we share the same profession, our career road maps may differ significantly. For Veterans, and Baby Boomers to a lesser degree, the end of WWII and the GI Bill prompted large numbers of men to migrate into teaching. The idea was to find a district in which you could establish roots and, if desired, move up by becoming a principal or superintendent. Job security was determined by virtue of one's accomplishments and tenure. This thinking worked fine when schools were more insular and lifetime employment was an unconditional guarantee.

On the other side of the coin is career security, a work ideal more aligned with Generation X and Millennial thinking. The premise here is that you build up a bank of knowledge and experiences so that no matter what bad things might happen, you are able to bounce back. Limitations on the portability of service credit prevents teachers from job hopping to the same degree as contemporaries in the private sector; however, young teachers today are far more nomadic than their Boomer colleagues. Loyalty to a school district doesn't resonate with Generation X in particular because they aren't convinced the system is committed to looking out for them over the long haul. While Veteran educators focused on building a legacy, and Boomers aspired to build stellar careers, Generation X and Millennials replacing them are more interested in building portable and parallel careers (Lancaster & Stillman, 2002).

As generational variances are examined, the catalyst for turbulence in schools becomes obvious. A typical clash of occupational values versus workplace reality is featured in Table 1.3, "Storyboard." The sagas of Doug and Evelyn demonstrate how cross-age dissent can bruise egos and wither relationships.

In Doug's case, he has used a communication style that is completely distasteful to the Generation X principal. Since this cohort sees things from a more cynical lens, clichés and hyperbole don't sit well with them.

A better strategy is for Doug to set expectations that define the right outcomes and then give the principal latitude in formulating steps to get there. Through weekly or biweekly conversations, Doug can offer constructive feedback that spotlights the principal's progress, rather than her failure. Members of Generation X often complain that their Boomer bosses are wishy-washy and give lip service to concepts such as *teamwork* and *empowerment* without practicing what they preach. So the most sensible way for Doug to guide the principal in laying out her plan is via a direct, yet individualistic, approach.

Taking a Veteran teacher like Evelyn by surprise is bad business. Maybe it's been convenient for this teacher to do her own thing because

Table 1.3   Storyboard

The Saga of Doug	The Saga of Evelyn
Doug, a 52-year-old assistant superintendent, is anxious to see test scores improve at an underperforming elementary school. Doug isn't convinced that the principal is doing all she can to push her staff and ratchet up the learning.	Evelyn, a 64-year-old English teacher, is asked to see the principal during her planning period on the last day of school. The Generation X principal matter-of-factly explains to Evelyn that declining enrollment has created a staffing surplus.
During a meeting, Doug tries to pump up the Generation X principal by urging her to "win one for the Gipper." The principal immediately scoffs at the metaphor. While Doug writes the principal off as uncooperative, the principal is convinced that everyone at the central office is self-righteous. It's obvious that Doug and the rest of his cronies don't have a clue about the challenges this overworked principal is facing!	Despite Evelyn's senior status, the principal believes her refusal to collaborate with colleagues is incompatible with the school's mission of working as a professional learning community. Thus, Evelyn is being transferred to a cross-town high school. Evelyn's response is laced with hurt and anger. "How can you do this to me?" she cries. "I opened this school in 1972 while you were still in diapers. This is my home!" Evelyn stomps out of the office and immediately contacts the union president. Her next step is to file a grievance.

no one has asked her to do otherwise. Before writing Evelyn off, the Generation X principal should slow down and look deeper into what is actually going on. She may be willing to contribute more and share her knowledge, but simply has never been asked. Outlining objectives that emphasize the experience and historical perspective of seasoned staff like Evelyn enables principals to pair them with younger faculty who see things through a different lens. Without checking up on Veteran faculty regularly and respectfully, administrators may unwittingly be permitting them to check out.

If leaders hope to load the big yellow bus with the right people and get the wrong people to move on, the career desires and distinctions of staff have to be considered. As aspirations are understood, forks can be drawn in the road to provide various routes for each employee. Asking teachers, "Where do you see yourself in five years?" "What kind of committees and projects do you prefer to work on?" "How would you like me to support you?" and "Is there anything that might get in your way of achieving these goals?" gives administrators insight into workplace ideals while also honoring age-based ambitions.

CONCLUSION: A CAUSE CÉLÈBRE

For the first time in the history of public education, four distinct age groups are working elbow to elbow. School systems require new tools for dealing with employees in age-sensitive ways. If intergenerational planning isn't embraced as a cause célèbre, the educational community may find itself on a demographic collision course. Consider why. First, schools are vulnerable to a mass exodus of employees entering their golden years. Yet, as Baby Boomers live longer, they aren't all that enamored with retirement. Older teachers and administrators, whose knowledge may not be as current as those coming straight out of the university, are inclined to have conflicting opinions about what's best for students.

Another cause for concern is that the working population between ages 25 and 54 will decline by 4.3 percent in the next five years, while the number of people age 55 and older will grow by 4.8 percent (BLS, 2004, June). A shrinking pool of job prospects will necessitate an even more aggressive recruitment campaign of immigrant and minority workers. Such an influx of diversity in the workplace certainly hastens the potential for conflict. Employers must openly acknowledge that other ages, other cultures, and other voices have as much claim on the world as they do.

Finally, escalating demands from parents have created a growing chasm between what is expected of local schools and what teachers may be willing or able to give. Veteran parents like Ward and June Cleaver considered it taboo to question authority. But now they have been replaced by Boomer dads and Generation X moms who see their obligation to their offspring as all encompassing. Clearly, such opposing personalities can drive a wedge into the core mission of building and sustaining collaborative learning communities.

The generational force orbiting schools is both powerful and subtle. Unlike other diversity factors such as race, gender, or ethnicity, cross-age differences affect every school employee every day. Unresolved discord leads to biases, dysfunctional relationships, and toxic cultures—all of which stand as a huge impediment to achievement.

Unfortunately, public institutions lag behind private industry when it comes to initiating harmonious, student-centered work environments. Educators have been accused of supporting mediocrity, being behind the times, and failing to accept the evolving needs of constituents. Through an emphasis on job flexibility, respectful relations, and appreciation for generational differences, exceptional school districts are turning the corner. Leaders who focus on their human capital as the blueprint for success can bridge the gap by knowing what makes their employees tick.

New Rules for the Sandbox

Schools have not been notably quick in adopting [new] technologies, and when they have, they have often used them merely to do old things in new ways.

—Philip Schlechty

To understand how generational turnings from the past influence schools in the present, we need to contemplate some of the defining events of the twentieth century that shaped public education. The industrial age marked the first major turning point for schools, as it forever altered the way work was done in America. Modern machines, coupled with advances in transportation and communication, propelled the Western world from an agrarian society to a manufacturing one.

This rise of industry sent businessmen and engineers on a mission to find "one best system" in which goods and materials could be mass-produced. In this single-system quest, jobs became highly repetitive and managers looked for any way possible to increase an employee's speed and output. Because it was thought that people themselves possessed little intrinsic motivation, the assembly line concept paid scant attention to the human side of an enterprise.

> **Generational Turning Points in Schools**
>
> 1. The Industrial Revolution
> 2. The Cold War
> 3. A Nation at Risk
> 4. Collective Bargaining

Prominent educators of the day were excited to transfer these innovative ideas from the factory floor to the classroom floor. Superintendent and National Education Association President William T. Harris wrote,

> Our schools are in a sense, factories, in which the raw materials (children) are to be shaped and fashioned in order to meet the various demands of life. The specifications for manufacturing come from the demands of the 20th century civilization, and it is the business of the school to build its pupils according to the specifications laid down. (DuFour & Eaker, 1998, p. 21)

Seemingly harsh by postmodern standards, these ideals shed light on the national mood that created the American educational system. Designed to produce the kind of workers industry needed, schools weren't expected to educate large numbers of children to very high levels. Teachers were left alone under a dome of privacy to deliver one-size-fits-all curricula. Students respected the teacher, didn't interrupt, and tried not to look foolish in front of their classmates. Principals roamed the hallways fixing operational dilemmas and keeping any incorrigibles in line. And superintendents and boards of education spent the bulk of their time adopting policies to preserve order and sameness.

COLORING WITHIN THE LINES

Although the original design of schools may no longer fit societal needs, educational institutions have been sluggish to change. Consider the decade-long debate that ensued after John Dewey's 1913 paper "Interest and Effort" gave rise to the progressive education movement (Tyler, 1986). Dewey's studies refuted the theory that material should be distasteful to students in order for them to acquire the discipline necessary to work hard on topics they found unpleasant. It wasn't until 1925 that teachers began to accept the idea that students' interests should be taken into account in planning their curriculum.

During the Depression, youth from the Veteran generation began to enroll in schools in large quantities because they were unable to find work. Although there was a move to reconstruct the general high school curriculum to accommodate the demands of Depression-era students, the ability to collaborate on a small or large scale was not a prerequisite for learning nor was it part of the national philosophy. Neither schools nor the workplace were set up so that people had to rely on one another to learn or accomplish tasks together. While a teacher's job was to deliver the prescribed course of study, he or she wasn't expected to worry much if pupils got it or liked it, or about what parents thought.

Examining school structures through a historical lens helps explain why older administrators and teachers have a harder time embracing new thinking frames such as shared leadership, differentiated instruction, teamwork, and parental involvement. After all, when Veterans and Baby Boomers went to school, teachers focused on right and wrong, good and bad. Students were compulsory attendees, not customers. Rules, routines, and repetition were in place to maintain stability and make sure everyone colored within the lines.

FROM SCHOOL TO WORK

With the primary mode of employment in the United States relying on manual labor throughout most of the twentieth century, an adult from the Veteran generation, and Baby Boomers to a lesser degree, could be functionally illiterate and still find decent work. Jobs that called for mathematical reasoning, analysis, and effective communication simply weren't in great demand. Since such skills weren't expected of the masses, schools were stratified to select and sort students on the likelihood of whether or not they would become "knowledge workers" (Schlechty, 1997).

The premise that all students could or should learn at high levels seemed inconceivable to Veteran educators. Teaching was anchored in the belief that intelligence was an innate skill, not something acquired or developed. Before the Soviets launched Sputnik in 1957, the purpose of schooling was simply to produce "basically literate" students who were morally and civically minded. However, once education was linked to issues concerning national defense and the economy, millions of dollars were poured into schools to retool math and science instruction. The cold war framed the second turning point for public education. The underlying goal was still to ensure children developed into productive citizens, but textbooks and inquiry-based models were ramped up significantly to improve students' ability to think.

Between 1945 and 1985, graduation rates climbed steadily from 40 to 73.9 percent (Schlechty, 1997). Schools were making remarkable progress in producing better-educated students. However, the 1983 release of *A Nation at Risk* set in motion a third defining moment for educators. The Commission on Excellence in Education took direct aim at schools, claiming, "if an unfriendly foreign power had attempted to impose on America the mediocre educational performance that exists today, we might well have viewed it as an act of war" (Bracey, 2003, p. 616). Secretary of Education

Terrel Bell convinced President Reagan that the document was full of good campaign material even though it didn't address any of the items on Reagan's educational agenda, such as restoring school prayer, vouchers, or tuition tax credit.

Prominent newspapers came to the defense of schools by calling the report "homily [hardly] worth more than a C in tenth grade English class" (Bracey, 2003, p. 616). But, the damage had been done. Veteran politicians who were responsible for creating the system were suddenly convinced the system was a mess. The only way to improve it, they said, was to usher in a new era of reform.

A lot of the hullabaloo surrounding *A Nation at Risk* stemmed from the stark reality that overseas competition with countries such as Japan had yanked the United States into a deep recession. By the early 1980s, unemployment had soared to 9.7 percent. Blue-collar jobs vanished overnight as automation and advancing technologies allowed entire factories to build things without employing a soul. In the manufacturing world, workers got tired and cranky, while machines powered on with infinite endurance.

Figure 2.1, "Employment by Major Industry Trends and Projections," shows how the nation's leap from the manufacturing age to the corporate age to the information age has impacted the job market. With the preponderance of occupations now in the service sector, new instructional models are needed to prepare Millennials, and those generations that will follow, to compete in a global marketplace. What may have been fine for our grandparents and parents isn't necessarily fine for our children and our children's children.

With changing priorities on how best to prepare students for life beyond high school, so, too, evolves the business of schooling. Learning, and the continuous ability to learn, is the new cornerstone of education (see Table 2.1, "Generational Hallmarks of Schooling"). A passport to college not only yields more lucrative employment opportunities, it paves the way for expanded job growth, career security, and a better quality of life.

As schools transition from "one-of-a-kind" industrial fortresses to "mastery-for-all" learning communities, approaches where differentiation adds little or no value can continue to be standardized. But where inefficiencies, redundancies, or a poor return on investment exist, the approaches should be reinvented so that students aren't forced into structures that no longer meet their needs. In the olden days, the citizenry simply had to be an informed body. Now, the citizenry must process and apply information in highly sophisticated ways.

Figure 2.1   Employment by Major Industry Trends and Projections

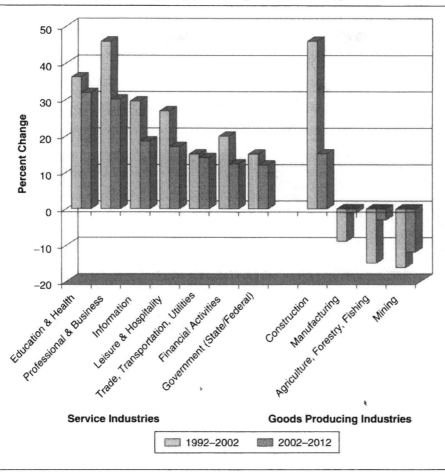

SOURCE: Bureau of Labor Statistics, www.bls.gov.

THE BIRTH OF ORGANIZED LABOR

Another influential by-product of the industrial age was the birth of organized labor. Abysmal and unsafe working conditions, low wages, and management's callous regard for human needs created the perfect fodder for an uprising. For teachers, who were primarily female and single, a contract in the good old days wasn't all that good. The job was neither glamorous nor well regarded. For a paltry $75 a month, a teacher's life was practically a one-way ticket to spinsterhood. Figure 2.2, "A Teacher's Contract in the Good Old Days," captures the essence of this demanding and restrictive profession.

Although the National Education Association (NEA) was founded in 1870 and the American Federation of Teachers (AFT) formed in 1916, it

Table 2.1   Generational Hallmarks of Schooling

Veterans: Born 1922–1943	Baby Boomers: Born 1944–1960	Generation X: Born 1960–1980	Millennials: Born 1980–2000
Grew up when children were to be seen, not heard; learned things the hard way; have immense faith in institutions such as church, school, and government	Rebelled from structured lives of Veteran parents; me-centered; better educated and more confident; challenge the status quo at every turn	Felt cheated by rebellious nature of Boomer parents; pragmatic and self-reliant; oriented toward "command thyself" mantra	Have traits similar to Veterans; intensely protected by parents and feel close to them; oriented toward "we will command everything" mantra
Schools prepare students to be book smart, industrialists	Schools prepare students to be inner-driven, idealists	Schools prepare students to be street smart, free agents	Schools prepare students to be rule-following, outward-driven, team players
High school diploma seen as badge of honor, but not critical for landing a good job	High school diploma no longer good enough; many Boomers go on to get higher degrees	High school diploma not critical for getting ahead; large numbers opt to take the GED	Not enough just to graduate at top of class; must be accepted to the best colleges and be #1 there, too

wasn't until President Kennedy signed Executive Order 10988 requiring federal managers to meet and confer with employee groups that unions gained momentum in the public sector. Activism in schools grew after NEA passed a resolution in the early 1960s urging school boards to negotiate directly with their members. With demonstrations and sit-ins dotting the national landscape, President Nixon was compelled to grant full bargaining rights to teachers in 1969. The opportunity for school employees to negotiate wages, hours, and terms and conditions of employment set in motion a fourth major turning point for public schools.

School leaders often wonder if it is possible to transfer an industrialized labor model built upon dissent and disagreement into a profession that needs sustained collaboration and cohesion. According to UCLA professor and author of *Making Schools Work* William Ouchi, teacher unions are faulted for corrupting public officials with their large campaign contributions, protecting bad teachers, fighting for salary increases irrespective of cuts to student programs, and handcuffing

Figure 2.2   A Teacher's Contract in the Good Old Days

- You will not marry during the term of your contract.
- You are not to keep company with men.
- You must be home between 8:00 p.m. and 6:00 a.m. unless in attendance at a school function.
- You may not loiter downtown in ice cream stores.
- You may not leave town at any time without the permission of the Chairman of the Trustees.
- You may not ride in a carriage or automobile with any man except your brother or your father.
- You may not smoke cigarettes.
- You may not drink beer, wine, or whiskey.
- You may not dress in bright colors.
- You may not dye your hair.
- You may not wear face powder, mascara, or paint your lips.
- You must wear at least two petticoats at all times.
- Your may not wear dresses more than two inches above the ankles.
- To keep the school room neat and clean you must:
  - ✓ Sweep the classroom floor at least once daily.
  - ✓ Scrub the classroom floor at least once a week with soap and water.
  - ✓ Clean the blackboards at least once daily.
  - ✓ Start the fire at 7:00 a.m. so that the room will be warm by 8:00 a.m. when the children arrive.

principals by taking away their authority to assign teachers where they are most needed (Ouchi, 2004). But it's unfair, says Ouchi, to place the bulk of the blame on unions. Antagonism, he believes, also stems from abusive management.

While unions shouldn't be allowed to bully principals, principals can't become emperors or empresses who demand that their subjects follow along blindly. The truth is that people from every cog on the generational wheel favor changes when they're in charge and rebuke changes when they're not. Administrators and teachers caught in a power struggle need to get into gear to become allies.

TRAILBLAZERS, PIONEERS, AND INDIANA JONES

The generational archetypes that pushed schools through nearly two decades of labor pains have to be understood as each side joins hands in search of common ground. The conventional heroes from the Veteran generation are proud that they were trailblazers in the labor movement. Fighting for dignity in the workplace gave Veteran teachers a shared purpose. This selfless cohort found strength in numbers and could stick together like glue. The struggle for uniform salaries, better teaching conditions, and job security made for a noble cause.

When Baby Boomers left college, they were malleable protégés for Veterans. If they were too young to participate directly in protests against the establishment, they had certainly grown up watching them on TV. "Norma Rae" Boomers, with a strong focus on self, were willing to fight to the death for what they believed in. Baby Boomers became the pioneers who used persuasion and persistence to establish unionized lunchrooms, orchestrate victorious elections, and put an end to teachers' suffering.

Rocked by inflation, unemployment, recession, and war, the United States weathered the largest, most publicized labor disputes in its history during the 1970s and early 1980s. Clashes between management and workers paralyzed business, commerce, and government from sea to shining sea (see sidebar, "Tumultuous Times"). Superintendents and boards of education were ill equipped to deal with such combativeness in the schoolhouse. The united front that had been taken for granted for so long quickly evaporated as local and state unions became more strident in their demands.

As collective bargaining turned into a cottage industry seemingly overnight, it was Generation X students who unwittingly got swept up in the fray. A September 1983 headline in *Education Week* announced, "13,500 Teachers Out on Strike in 38 Districts." Despite AFT president

---

Tumultuous Times

- **1970:** The first mass work stoppage in U.S. history occurs as 210,000 postal workers walk off the job. Four different railroad unions coordinate a one-day nationwide strike that same year.
- **1971:** Two longshoreman strikes close every major port on the East, West, and Gulf coasts. Over 400,000 members of the Communications Workers of America silence Ma Bell for a week.
- **1975:** In Pennsylvania, 80,000 state workers organize the first strike by public employees. Teacher strikes soon follow in 241 school districts.
- **1977:** The longest strike in history is launched by 78 miners.
- **1979:** Nearly a quarter million long- and short-haul truckers stay off the roads.
- **1981:** Some 13,000 air traffic controllers abandon their towers, causing the cancellation of 6,000 commercial flights. Those who refuse to follow President Reagan's edict to return to work within 48 hours are fired.

SOURCE: Bureau of Labor Statistics, 2001.

Albert Shanker pronouncing it a relatively calm school opening, 225,000 youngsters arrived for their first day of class only to discover Ms. Jones had played hooky.

The good news is that schools have experienced more tranquility in recent history. While there were 241 nationwide teachers' strikes in 1975, that number plummeted to 99 in 1991 and dropped to a mere 15 in 2003 (Hess, 2005). The decline is attributed to changes in state laws prohibiting strikes coupled with a greater understanding on the part of school boards and superintendents for teachers to play a key role in their destiny.

Perhaps a lesser known factor also weighing in on these kinder, gentler times is the notion that teachers from Generation X aren't consumed by the same sense of duty as Veterans nor do they gravitate toward the idealism Boomers find so compelling. With an Indiana Jones spirit, Generation X teachers live by their wits and roam through their careers looking for an adrenaline rush. They are adventurous, willing to take risks in the classroom, and less fearful of things such as test scores or average yearly progress. Generation X staff members have the freedom and confidence to go elsewhere if things don't work out.

Baby Boomers, on the other hand, are competitive, like to retain control of their curriculum, and strive to teach their way. Caught up in their own self-interests and priorities, the thought of developing common assessments or having test scores published in the local newspaper can make a Boomer jittery. Unions offer up protection from excessive scrutiny or unwanted criticism.

As Millennial teachers step aboard, they maintain characteristics similar to Generation X in their acceptance of responsibility for achievement. Having been raised during the height of the standards and accountability movement, they put tremendous pressure on themselves to succeed and don't want to make mistakes. What's different, though, is that Millennials trust institutions in ways Generation X and Baby Boomers would never dream of.

THE NEUTRAL ZONE

Lurking in the minds of seasoned teachers may be the feeling that past injustices can only be remedied through an adversarial campaign. Therefore, when working with older staff, any decisions about the future should be contemplated within the context of the past. Veterans and Baby Boomers don't fight for change, but instead fiercely lobby to maintain the status quo. It was through sweat and sacrifice they were able to break through the bureaucracy to earn decent pay, greater autonomy, and better working conditions.

It should come as no surprise that Baby Boomers have not responded well to concepts such as site-based management and shared decision making. In their heart of hearts, they believe such duties rest with the administration. And when things go awry, it is much easier to blame the principal than it is to take responsibility themselves. Conversely, older superintendents and principals have a hard time relinquishing information and control to subordinates. Beneath it all, they see the hierarchy as a safe, predictable structure to manage. Unless these underlying values are addressed, old wounds will fester and scars will deepen, leaving students the victims of the chasm.

Finding the neutral zone requires generational savvy. The following tips will help school leaders use calculated sensitivity to tackle complex issues and move "seniors" forward.

FINDING THE NEUTRAL ZONE WITH "SENIORS"

• **Prove the necessity for change in terms of months and years, not weeks.** Veterans and Baby Boomers are in it for the long haul, especially if plans for getting there are woven into a captivating story. Appeal to their sense of loyalty and dedication by revisiting where the workplace has been in relation to where it's going. Emphasize big-picture thinking.

• **Don't denigrate the past.** The best way to nudge older faculty members into the future is to build upon the past. If you ridicule the old ways, you are essentially demeaning the people who were responsible for establishing them. To make lasting improvements, frame ideas for change around the existing culture.

• **Use the personal touch.** Veterans want to work in places with living human beings. They've been slow to respond to voicemail, e-mail, and homework hotlines primarily because they enjoy socializing. In the good old days, when there was more time to kill, it was best not to show too much initiative. It could earn you more work. It is likely Veterans and older Boomers (not Generation X or Millennials) who spend prep periods hanging out at the secretary's desk, chatting with the custodian, or dropping in on a neighbor next door.

• **Unload old baggage.** Try to understand which individuals are most affected by changes. Ask questions such as, "What's different this year than last year or the year before?" "What have you lost or given up?" "Is it possible to reach this point by . . . ?" and "How can I help you get there?" As unresolved issues are recognized, the healing process gets underway.

- **Innovate judiciously.** Senior teachers become cynical when new concepts are out of their league or are viewed as repackaged failures of the past. From their perspective, they've "been there, done that." Without simplifying innovations or laying out ideas in a cogent manner, older faculty members will become conscientious objectors.

- **Help them pass the torch.** Veterans and Baby Boomers have a treasure trove of knowledge to be kindled before their flame is extinguished. They are proud to be associated with organizations that strive to be number one. Play up this role of honored historian by emphasizing the need to take newcomers under their wing and share their wisdom. When senior teachers pass the torch to protégés, their own legacy is preserved.

Once the moral fibers of senior teachers are sewn, turn your attention to the other end of the age spectrum. While Baby Boomers demand *equality* for all, Generation X is concerned with *equity* for all. For example, a 2003 Public Agenda survey revealed that 55 percent of new teachers think that districts should be able to use criteria other than years of experience and education to financially reward teachers, while only 33 percent of veteran teachers agreed with this practice (Farkas, Johnson, & Duffett, 2003). Two in three respondents said teachers who work harder and put in additional time and effort should be paid more, especially in areas where shortages exist. Members of Generation X question why they should exert tremendous energy when older colleagues are allowed to be slackers.

Another bone of contention for the teaching neophyte is the requirement that he or she must cough up an equal share of union dues despite being the first one tossed overboard during a layoff or staffing surplus. Only 19 percent of the respondents in the Public Agenda survey felt their national association accurately reflected their values and preferences. Generation X and Millennials don't share the same homogenized views about organized labor as older colleagues, nor are they willing to join things the way their parents or grandparents did—especially if they don't see anything in it for themselves.

The Florida Education Association (FEA) serves as a poignant example of this waning interest in union participation. While two-thirds of the state's teachers with 20-plus years of service belong to the union, only a third on the job for five years or less are members (Hegarty & Gilmer, 2002). Minimizing seniority's impact on novices will bring the generations closer together. On the other hand, using archaic reasoning with this younger crowd is bound to cause frustration and apathy.

Figure 2.3   Personal Rx: Setting the Pace

- Have I myself accepted the reality that nonstop change is inevitable or am I still thinking "this too shall pass"?
- Have I studied the changes in my school to see which are directly tied to our major district objectives?
- Am I careful not to introduce extra, unrelated changes while teachers are still struggling to respond to huge transitions from before?
- Have I created a clear picture of the change and found ways to communicate it effectively?
- Have I helped staff unload old baggage and/or given them time to grieve when sacred cows are eliminated?
- Have I mapped out a blueprint for success to help our school stay on course?
- Do I connect the dots by showing teachers how changes this year are linked to last year and woven into what will happen next year?
- Do I include worst case scenarios with my change agenda to forecast future results?
- Have I given each staff member a tangible way to contribute so that the work is shared and everyone is a part of the process?
- Am I planning and managing the transition from "occasional change" to "change as the norm" and encouraging others to do the same?

The "us against them" mentality, which was an awakening of sorts for the "boomerocracy," doesn't hold the same appeal with Generation X, who lived through the turmoil. Furthermore, it's unlikely that attitudes will change drastically with a Millennial-dominated workforce, since this group is known to be more indecisive, subtle, and eager to avoid conflict.

So how do educational leaders push for change while protecting the generational comfort zone that gives each staff member a sense of pride, stability, and accomplishment? Just because something is old, does that mean it's bad, and if something is new, does that mean it's good? If change is a journey, is it possible to get cross-age groups to pack up their suitcases and leave home at the same time?

Use the "Personal Rx: Setting the Pace" in Figure 2.3 to set the pace. Start by isolating the changes most likely to have the greatest impact on achievement and then decide the best order in which to do things. The tempo should be fast enough so that younger employees don't lose interest, while slow enough so that older employees aren't overwhelmed.

THAT WAS THEN, THIS IS NOW

Vastly different social and economic times call for vastly different instructional models. As schools transition from adult-centered networks to student-centered ones, old style tactics may no longer mesh with new-style learning (See Table 2.2, "Schools Then, Schools Now").

Table 2.2   Schools Then, Schools Now

Schools Then	Schools Now
• What was taught • Chapters covered; workbooks completed • Textbook drives curriculum • Bell-shaped curve • One chance to succeed • Paper-and-pencil tasks • Whole-class instruction; teach to the middle • Teachers talk, students listen • Passive learning • Teach it one way • Assess after it's taught • Basics for all; thinking for the gifted • One subject at a time • What product will be created? • Is this a good lesson? • Focus on activities	• What is learned • Several resources; use only what's needed • Assessment drives curriculum • Mastery of standards • Multiple chances to succeed • Performance-based tasks • Flexible group instruction; differentiate to reach the top, middle, and bottom • Students talk, teachers listen • Active learning • Teach it many ways • Assess before, during, and after it's taught • Basics and thinking for everyone • Integrated subjects throughout the day • What process will be created? • Is this the right lesson? • Focus on results

SOURCE: Adapted from Rutherford, P. (2002). *Instruction for all students.* Alexandria, PA: Just ASK Publications. Reprinted with permission.

For education to serve as the engine of democracy, schools have to run on four generational cylinders. Anyone who cares about the profession knows there is little tolerance among the public or lawmakers for petty bickering and whining. Disagreements have to be handled in a civil, constructive way with the goal of a speedy resolution. If teachers and administrators become paralyzed by outdated traditions or polarized by bitter disputes, taxpayers may start asking for a refund.

CONCLUSION: LET GO OF THE QUO

To merge tradition with innovation, leaders must nudge teachers along without bulldozing them over. Although timed tests, weekly spelling bees, and true/false exams may have been adequate for earlier generations, more is needed for today's learner. A displaced factory worker simply cannot transition into a knowledge or service job the way farmers and domestic laborers did a century ago. Without every student having the chance to earn a living wage in a knowledge-based economy, segments of the population shall remain excluded from its benefits. High-impact schools are turning the corner by preparing students for life beyond high school, instead of just getting them ready for graduation day.

Older teachers who helped champion civil rights and due process are being replaced by champions of civic duty and social conscience. As Baby Boomers reach their pinnacle of power, they are anxious to leave their mark before fading into the sunset. On the flip side of the coin are Generation Xers and Millennials, who maintain unconventional attitudes about work. Competence is valued over cronyism, longevity, and sacred traditions. Younger teachers rely on a kaleidoscope lens to see and do things differently.

Clashes between Baby Boomers and Generation X and Generation X and Millennials will likely escalate over the next few years. Leaders seeking change should follow a nonlinear path to deliver the message and find equilibrium. Understanding the generational hubs and networks suspended throughout the hierarchy is tantamount to bridging the cross-age divide and leaving the status quo behind.

Cross-Age Connections in a Learning Community

Quality teaching requires strong professional learning communities. Collegial interchange, not isolation, must become the norm for teachers.

—National Commission on Excellence in Elementary Teacher Prep (2003)

As the national spotlight remains fixed on public education, the cycle of reform continues in our schools. With such glaring attention, it's easy for educational leaders to become confused and end up fixing the wrong things. "Déjà vu" reform may actually kill creativity and stall progress if we're not careful.

But there are some measures underway that seem to be lighthouses for school improvement. One such effort is the professional learning community (PLC) movement. In fact, the term PLC has become so ubiquitous that almost every new approach to beef up learning makes reference to it, sometimes without much regard for the elements that are essential to its development. Principals use the words to describe various combinations of team effort. Again, if educators are not careful, the concept, like others that have come before, could lose all meaning.

A unifying component of the learning community model is collaboration. Representing more than just a series of practices, PLC principles rest upon the ideals, assumptions, and expectations governing how people in a school work together. Unfortunately, most schools are still characterized by teacher isolation and free agency. Traditional high schools have been described as a collection of independent contractors united only by a common parking lot (DuFour, Eaker, & DuFour, 2005).

A major goal in the design of a learning community is facilitating a culture of collaboration within a setting that is complicated by the cross-age diversity of most teams. Such grade-level or departmental teams are likely to consist of varying mixtures of Veterans, Baby Boomers, Generation X, and even Millennials, as noted in the preceding chapters, all with unique ways of communicating and divergent belief systems.

Professional learning communities are places where every generation is both a teacher and learner. Transforming schools into PLCs cannot be left to chance. Without focused leadership to build and fortify sturdy pillars of collaboration, meaningful teamwork will be talked about but seldom practiced.

INTERGENERATIONAL CHEMISTRY IN A PLC

America's schools are, for the most part, led by Baby Boomers. The principal's office and key district-level positions are mainly occupied by those who grew up in the post–World War II boom and who will continue to fill these seats well into 2012. Schools, however, are full of Generation X teachers and aspiring administrators who perceive things much differently than their Boomer bosses. If the collaborative team is the engine of a professional learning community, the already daunting task of creating and sustaining cohesion among an entire workforce is further exacerbated by the mixed nature of most groups.

Why even be concerned about the obvious reality that most school teams will comprise members from different generations? First and foremost, learning communities rely on administrators, departments, grade levels, and interdisciplinary groups to get the work done. Decisions in these settings are inclusive, rather than top down. The problem schools run into is that the values and work ethic of Generation X differ so significantly from Baby Boomers that, if not addressed, it is almost impossible to develop the cooperative and interdependent relationships necessary to have a viable learning community.

Since professional learning communities depend on far more than comfortable collegiality, trick trading, or debating mundane issues such as the duty schedule, differences must be understood and talked about in order for the PLC engine to purr. By studying the intergenerational chemistry of the staff as a whole, many solutions for the challenges experienced in schools can be found. On the other hand, ignoring irregularities may lead to a meltdown.

At the heart of the clash between Generation X and Baby Boomers are the issues of balance with work and the rest of life. Boomers believe it is their mission to make a difference in the world. They have revolutionized the meaning of career, productivity, and achievement—quite often at the expense of personal relationships. Many Boomers are known to define their very existence by their job and professional success.

This "live to work" ethos lies in stark contrast to that of Generation X, for whom the phrase "work to live" has taken on new meaning. Many children raised themselves, creating an entire population of adults accustomed to getting things done on their own.

While growing up in the 1970s, Generation X was surrounded by bumper stickers, posters, and public service announcements urging the nation to adopt the ZPG (zero population growth) philosophy. Slogans such as "the pill in time saves nine" didn't impress upon young people that they were wanted or deserving of much attention. As a result, Generation X tends to be unwilling to collaborate in the same manner as their Boomer bosses or Boomer coworkers. Furthermore, they place great emphasis on finding balance and enjoyment in life, making certain that work doesn't compromise their extensive outside interests.

What does all this mean for school leaders attempting to bridge the generational divide? Is there a way to enmesh multiage teams throughout a campus? Leaders must first study these differences and then appeal separately to the desires and values of each group. Baby Boomers will respond best to frequent public recognition of their contributions and sacrifices. They crave and expect the opportunity to give input before decisions are made. While Generation X doesn't need the public acclaim, they do need adequate space to get the job done efficiently so that they can move on to more important roles in their life.

KNOW YOUR LINEUP

Since Baby Boomers are good at relationships, aim to please, and are practiced team players, they are perfect to take charge of tasks that require consensus building and the facilitation of meetings (Ansoorian, Good, & Samuelson, 2003). Conversely, Generation X employees, with all their technical literacy and creative juices, are well suited to work alone on projects or activities that require analytical expertise or research. The Generation X team member can then share the results of his or her work with colleagues, thereby allowing the group to jointly decide where to go from there. As school teams gather in September to set norms, an awareness of generational differences should be factored into discussions about how tasks might be assigned and completed throughout the year.

Of course, all of this differentiation holds the possibility of breeding resentment and even conflict. Baby Boomers may get upset with Generation X's work ethic and begrudge them for moving up the career ladder without as much personal sacrifice or paying their dues. Generation X may view Baby Boomer colleagues as stuck in their ways and unwilling to let go of the power they have amassed after years of being workaholics. Baby Boomers may become frustrated by the lack of commitment and unhurried pace Generation X sets in finishing assignments. Generation X may scoff at a Baby Boomer's overzealous demeanor in seeing a project to fruition and lapping up the rewards like a thirsty Saint Bernard.

As with so much in life, communication is key. Leaders of professional learning communities have to learn to accept and appreciate the opposing needs of Baby Boomers and Generation X. For a school's motor to run smoothly and powerfully, principals and coadministrators should openly acknowledge differences and model strategies to deal with them. The idea is to create teams that effectively use and maximize the strengths of one another, no matter what generation they happen to come from.

The intergenerational dialogue so vital to authentic teamwork does not necessarily come naturally to teachers. Because they spend the entire day talking to students, the assumption is that communication is something teachers do well. In a way, such behavior is precisely why the issue of communication has to be addressed. The true workplace realities are noted below (Bamburg, n.d.):

Nowhere in the formal preparation and training of teachers is a significant amount of time invested in learning how to work with adults.

Teachers spend the majority of their day isolated from one another.

The collegial conversations teachers do end up having tend to be short and focused on resolving an immediate dilemma or need.

A degree of adult denial and dysfunction is tolerated in schools mainly because all the grown-ups (teachers and administrators) have yet to master this fine art of working together.

"Developing a staff's capabilities for talking together professionally is no panacea, but it may represent one of the single most significant investments that faculties can make for student learning" (Garmston &

Wellman, 1999, p. 52). It is the principal's job to make it clear that working together is not negotiable. Faculty members across generations have to be focused on the mission, goals, roles, and responsibilities inherent in the work of educating children.

A school leader has to know his or her lineup in order to bridge the understanding gap that may be preventing staff from joining forces. The sidebar "Essential Strategies to Focus School Teams" outlines techniques that can remove age-based prejudgments that sometimes hinder collaboration.

Essential Strategies to Focus School Teams

1. Reignite the team
2. Define the team's mission
3. Clarify the group's work
4. Define each member's role
5. Leverage uniqueness

SOURCE: From *Managing the Generation Mix* by Carolyn Martin and Bruce Tulgan, copyright © 2002. Reprinted by permission of the publisher, HRD Press, Amherst, MA, (800) 822-2801, www.hrdpress.com

- Reignite the team: One of the classic complaints heard from employees of all ages is, "What is the meeting for—what are we supposed to do?" It is important to the success of intergenerational teams to answer the following questions and use the answers to focus their work together:
  1. Is our school's mission meaningful enough to motivate us to contribute our best each and every day? If not, why not? What would it take to make it so?
  2. Has the real mission of our school changed over time? Does it need revision?
  3. How can we redefine our school and/or team mission so we can really buy into it?
  4. Vision is about the future, but mission is about right now. Most schools have written the obligatory, mostly ignored, mission statement. When was the last time you pulled yours out, dusted it off, and engaged people in a lively conversation about the purpose and values that actually drive the work being done right now?

- Define the team's mission: When a grade level or department is about to consider a specific project related to student learning, it is important to clarify exactly what they are attempting to accomplish. Here are some questions that might be posed:
  1. Why are we focusing on this specific project or task?
  2. What special qualifications do our team members possess relative to this project?

    3. What might be the impact on student learning if our team doesn't attempt this project?

- Clarify the group's work: Once the team has defined its mission, the focus can turn to the project at hand. Inquiries include the following:
  1. What specific tasks have to be accomplished to complete the project?
  2. In what order will these tasks be undertaken and what are the deadlines?
  3. How will success be measured?
  4. What are the key guidelines to be observed?

Assignments should be those that are meaningful, not just the same recycled activities that have always been done. Reevaluate each exercise or task to identify which things are truly necessary, which are nice, and which can be let go. Figure 3.1, "The Scope of Our Team's Work," provides a template to help teams outline priorities, tasks, and timelines.

- Define each member's role: Once people are clear about the work to be done, decide who will play what role on the team. This is where an understanding of the generational differences outlined in Chapter 1 can support participant buy-in and the eventual successful completion of the project or task. Few things weaken a team faster than unclear or undefined roles or failure to take into account the individual skills and intrinsic motivation of each member. Team members should answer the following:
  1. What resources of time, energy, skills, knowledge, and talent will each person contribute to the effort?

Figure 3.1   The Scope of Our Team's Work

Projects, Tasks, and Responsibilities	Goals and Deadlines	Guidelines	Are Guidelines Negotiable?

SOURCE: From *Managing the Generation Mix* by Carolyn Martin and Bruce Tulgan, copyright © 2002. Reprinted by permission of the publisher, HRD Press, Amherst, MA, (800) 822-2801, www.hrdpress.com

2. How can we consult effectively to get the work done?
3. Who is best suited to do what?
4. What starring roles and what supporting roles is each person willing to play?

Successful sports teams demand individual excellence, no matter what position an athlete plays. When called upon, a bench player needs to contribute 100 percent just like the starter. In fact, the most successful teams have deep benches as well as a lineup of stars. Teams need individuals who can assist as well as score, who can follow as well as lead. Teamwork in a PLC is definitely not a spectator event.

- Leverage uniqueness: Help team members get started quickly and discard excess baggage by using a round-table approach whereby each member is given equal time to share views on three key issues:
  1. The talents, skills, knowledge, and experience that he or she brings to the table
  2. Areas where individual improvement in performance is possible in the near future
  3. The type of support desired in terms of coaching, training, or mentoring

In turn, the group leader should openly affirm the strengths of each participant by offering specific examples of how these strengths have been used in accomplishing designated tasks. Suggestions can then be provided to enlist others in sharing their expertise and coaching teammates.

A CASE IN POINT

One Ohio school district has the current distinction of being the fastest growing in the state. Situated in burgeoning Delaware County near Columbus, it was once an agricultural community. Now, strip malls and housing tracts have gobbled up farmland. Twelve years ago, the district housed all of its students in a single building. However, in five short years, it doubled in size and opened six brand new campuses. Maintaining continuous improvement amid such rapid growth is a huge challenge, and one increasingly familiar to school districts throughout America.

The district has a core group of teachers, Veterans and Baby Boomers, who have been together for decades. Nostalgically, these pioneers remember when they were like a family in the same building. The assistant director of curriculum and instruction shared that when the first new building opened, many of the core teachers went through a grieving process from the loss of being separated.

As might be expected, most of the ninety-some new teachers hired each year are from Generation X. Newcomers have to quickly be assimilated into the district's curriculum, culture, and plans for improvement. Art Counts, a 26-year Veteran art teacher, breaks down the employee mix into three distinct groups—teachers with less than 12 years experience, teachers with 12 to 25 years, and teachers with more than 25 years (Gordon, 2005, February).

Seasoned faculty members like Counts see it as their job to familiarize first-year teachers with the values and traditions of the organization. He believes that new teachers must have high expectations for students and learn to nurture the total child. Counts encourages "newbies" to become involved with the students as a coach or club advisor so that they get to know them on a different level.

Of course, the kind of mentoring Mr. Counts describes can be greatly improved when everyone has some awareness of how the generations may vary in their outlook on life and work. For example, the district now has many staff members with fewer than 12 years in the district. Some are from other communities and some are brand new to teaching. Both groups represent a blend of Generation X and Millennials.

Liz McCullough, a high school science teacher, and Lesley Lawlis, a teacher working with gifted children at the feeder middle school, rave about the support they received from administrators and colleagues when they first arrived. A structured induction program, with trained mentors, offers newcomers whatever is needed in their inaugural years. Such formalized support is further enhanced by an awareness and knowledge of how younger and older teachers differ. Lawlis summed up the benefit of this induction, "Although I am relatively new, I feel valued and integrated into the culture of the school" (Gordon, 2005, February, p. 7).

One way to deal with workplace changes such as those described in the preceding paragraphs is for principals to orchestrate a generational summit. The purpose of such an event is to remove walls and replace them with bridges. Through a series of breakout sessions described in the "Cross-Age Colloquium" in Table 3.1, teachers have the chance to share insights, raise awareness, and confront any elephants in the room.

Learning more about the beliefs and uniqueness of each generation builds stable team relationships, enhances group identity, and allows tasks to be accomplished without significant setbacks. Without the orchestration of such rich dialogue about age diversity, it may be next to impossible for a principal to sustain schoolwide collaboration over the long haul.

Table 3.1   Cross-Age Colloquium: Program Overview

Part One *Like Generation Groups*	Part Two *Mixed Generation Groups*
Getting Started: Have teachers meet in like generational groups to discuss the questions below. Responses can be recorded on chart paper. Allow 15–20 minutes for the brainstorming and 20 minutes for the whole group to share their thoughts: • What are some of the characteristics our generation has in common? • What are some of the distinguishing characteristics among other generations? • What do we like about working with others who share the same generational coding? • What frustrates us about working with other generations who simply can't see things our way?	***Getting Started:*** Have teachers meet in mixed generational groups to discuss the questions below. Responses can be recorded on chart paper. Allow 15–20 minutes for the brainstorming and 20 minutes for the whole group to share their thoughts: • What were your expectations about a career when you first began teaching? • How have these expectations changed? • How are you dealing with workplace changes as they relate to student learning? • What have you learned about yourself by participating in these discussions?
Points of Emphasis: If we are going to create a strong team that gets the best work done every day, our task is to maximize the contributions each person in the group makes. We respect and honor our differences and approach them not as a reason for conflict, but as a springboard for learning, productivity, and innovation.	***Points of Emphasis:*** Since we are all living during this fast-paced, often unpredictable moment in history, no single generation has a monopoly on defining the new workplace—not Veterans or Boomers who hold top positions, nor Generation X with all their techno-savvy and independence. Everyone, regardless of age, has to be flexible, entrepreneurial knowledge workers. Everyone must sharpen their skills and talents to get the best work done every day.
Afterthought: Every generation can benefit from the perspectives and strengths of others. Veterans usually have the most experience, the best institutional memory, and the highest degree of wisdom. Generation X and Millennials bring fresh ideas and energy to the table. Baby Boomers bridge the gap between the past and the future. They relate to both the perspective of the most experienced people and the innovative impulses of the youngest on the team.	***Afterthought:*** Each generation is navigating through life's fast-paced terrain, but it can look quite different from each lane. Veterans typically experience these changes—globalization, technology, restructuring—as revolutionary; everything about work is changing. For Generation X and Millennials, the changes are exciting. Every change is an opportunity to seize and turn into one's own personal proving ground. The Boomer majority in the middle tends to feel the most conflicted about the new workplace.

(Continued)

Table 3.1 (Continued)

Part Three *Department, Grade-Level, or Project Teams*	*Part Four: Self-Reflection* **Principals, Assistant Principals, Team Leaders**
Getting Started: In advance of the session, distribute a selected article on the growing generational mix in the American workplace. Several articles are available on the Internet and in professional journals. Suggested readings include the following: ✓ Ansoorian, A., Good, P., & Samuelson, D. (2003, May–June). Managing generational differences. *Leadership, 32*(5) 34–36 ✓ Learner, N. (2002, May 6). When generations meet on the job. *Christian Science Monitor.* Available at http://www.csmonitor.com/ ✓ Lovely, S. (2005, September). Creating synergy in the schoolhouse. *The School Administrator, 8*(62) 30–34 ✓ Raines, C. (1999). The boomers and the Xers. *Claire Raines & Associates.* Available at http://www.generationsatwork.com/articles.htm ✓ Strauss, W. (2005, September). Talking about their generation. *The School Administrator. 8*(62) 10–14 Discuss the following questions about the article: • What "aha" resonated with you as you read this article? • Is there a way to tie this information to the development and structure of our department or grade-level team? • How has your thinking changed as a result of our cross-age colloquium?	**Getting Started:** A key component in managing a multigenerational workforce is to understand yourself and how your own generational traits impact your leadership style. Once you have had an opportunity to participate in the colloquium, sit down and reflect on the following: • What do I believe are the most important attributes a teacher should have? • What symbols of recognition do I hold important? • What balance do I maintain between work and personal life? • What judgments do I make about other people when they don't comport to these ideals? • What characteristics of other generations trigger frustration and disappointment in me? • Am I an active listener willing to make an effort to understand why teachers do what they do? • Do I have a strong sense of vision and do I communicate this vision to everyone? • Do I feel the need to be steadfastly correct or do I exhibit a flexible leadership style for handling the cross-age diversity in our school?
Points of Emphasis: There are many dimensions to diversity. Author Claire Raines has likened it to sorting a deck of cards. A deck of cards can be divided by color, number, suit, and so forth. If we look at our school staff like a deck of cards, we can be sorted in many ways—two stacks by gender or several stacks by ethnicity, countries of origin, age, and so forth. Each time the cards are sorted and we explore how the stacks are different and similar, we get a broader perspective of every card, as well as the complete deck of 52.	**Points of Emphasis:** Once you have identified your own views about work ethic, needs, and motivating factors, ask yourself whether it is possible to modify your approach to accommodate different generational viewpoints. Continue to look for ways to provide the people you lead with opportunities to introduce new ideas and be a part of the decision-making process. Find ways for them to contribute that match their level of comfort and confidence.
Afterthought: During the discussion, the principal and coadministrators should circulate among the groups to listen to the dialogue and get a sense of how team members might play off one another and where they might clash. This is helpful for organizing group work and team goals in the future.	**Afterthought:** Don't get caught up in titles or the power of your position. Professional learning communities aren't about who's where on the organizational chart, who has more degrees lining the wall, or who runs around doing whatever the principal says.

CONCLUSION: AGELESS EXCELLENCE

Your team's discussions of generational issues will be an eye-opener. It isn't the panacea for solving all future misunderstandings, but it will begin to clear the air and alter assumptions. However, helping people understand their differences and uniqueness is only the beginning. If a leader stops there, he or she is left with, "Now that we understand one another, let's be polite and make nice." That works—as it does for all diversity issues—but only up to a point.

Administrators also have to steer their team toward the finish line—improved results in student achievement reached collaboratively and interdependently. Once age is no longer an issue, the willingness and ability of each team member to leverage his or her strengths and contributions becomes the impetus for action.

The best generational leaders maximize each employee's productivity by mastering three core competencies: focus, communication, and customization. They focus members on the team's mission and goals as well as the roles they will play to accomplish them. They design easy-to-use communication systems that provide information and resources just in time, all the time. Finally, they keep faculty engaged by customizing incentives (release time vs. additional assignment pay) to fit the needs of a multiage team.

How team members converse is just as significant as what they converse about. When teachers talk about important topics, it fosters shared commitment and shared action. To build a professional learning community that exudes ageless excellence, generational biases have to be erased so that pathways to collaboration can be drawn. It's not about right or wrong, your way or my way. It's about putting students' learning needs and interests above all else.

Recruitment Renaissance

Give It to 'Em Their Way

When I recruit people, I don't look at them for the job that we're hiring them for. I want to see if they have the capability to go two or three jobs beyond that.

—Ed Gilbert, West Group Publishing

Some of the toughest recruitment battles being waged in the United States are among school districts. While Millennials warm every classroom seat, there is growing competition to find qualified and capable adults to teach them.

In California, a burgeoning population coupled with the statewide implementation of class size reduction has spawned 200,000 new teaching positions since 1996 (CSR Research Consortium, 2002). In Minneapolis, 65 percent of the city's teaching force has fewer than five years of experience (Lancaster & Stillman, 2002). And *Viva Las Vegas!* has taken on a whole new meaning in Nevada, where 1,500 to 2,000 teachers are hired annually. As the fastest growing district in the nation, Clark County Schools expect to add another 500 administrators to their roster by the end of the decade. With jobs aplenty, school districts across America must mine and manage every generation to fill the void.

Educators are among an older-than-average workforce, a situation that has been further exacerbated by successive years of hiring slowdowns and freezes, early retirement incentives, and a large number of young people leaving the profession. In 1981, for instance, the average age of teachers in the United States was 37. But, within 20 years, that average had jumped to age 46 (National Center for Educational Statistics, 2003).

When looking at principal demographics, retirements aren't the only concern. According to a recent RAND study, beginners are getting older, too. In 1988, 38 percent of all new principals were under age 40. But by the year 2000, that figure had dropped to 12 percent (RAND Education, 2003). Rookies also spend fewer years on the job than their predecessors, which is especially disturbing given principals don't stick around much past age 55. Clearly, the recruitment pickings are getting slimmer all the way around.

With the lion's share of the work-age population shrinking, harvesting the next generation of school employees isn't just nice to do, it is absolutely essential. Drawing newcomers into teaching, while encouraging the not-so-over-the-hill 59ers to stick around a bit longer, is paramount. Designing a succession plan to identify and inspire talented teacher leaders with strong administrative potential makes good business sense, too. Organizations that develop a high-quality workforce are building stock in their future. Those that dismiss or ignore the need to prepare tomorrow's employees today will undoubtedly wind up with the leftovers.

GENERATIONAL FORECASTING

School districts need the capacity to respond to changing market conditions, whether this means staffing up because of enrollment growth, staffing down because of declining birth rates, or staffing out because of hard-to-fill positions. Regardless of your current employment situation, waiting passively for candidates to show up on your doorstep is akin to waiting for a blizzard and then deciding to shop for a winter coat. Once you finally make it over to Filene's Basement, the merchandise is well picked over. Consider the dichotomy of these two school districts as they scramble for solutions to the growing principal shortage:

A group of self-selected principal prospects decide to take a dip in the River of School Leadership. Soon, the fast-moving current sweeps the prospects away as the superintendent and trustees watch helplessly from the muddy banks. In the leadership-challenged district, half-hearted attempts to save them consist of throwing in mentors who hurriedly try to teach the fundamentals of management. A few wannabes are strong enough to grab hold. But most float on by.

On the other side of the river, the leadership-able district sends a team of scouts upstream to see what's causing their folks to fall in. As the principals-in-the-making are pulled safely ashore downstream, their skills are assessed. The superintendent and key staff install safety netting and re-contour the landscape upstream. A rescue force comprising seasoned principals is commissioned to bring back anyone frightened off by the commotion. Obviously, the leadership-able district knows that without protecting their precious resources, they'll drown.

SOURCE: From Lovely, S. (2004). *Staffing the Principalship*, p. 124. Reprinted by permission. The Association for Supervision and Curriculum Development is a worldwide community of educators advocating sound policies and sharing best practices to achieve the success of each learner. To learn more, visit ASCD at www.ascd.org

In simple terms, generational forecasting involves targeting prospective recruits in new ways. It means finding a niche for people and tapping into their occupational aspirations and potential. The goal is to have a viable pool of Millennials and Generation X waiting in the wings as Baby Boomers and Veterans make their exit. Getting the process underway consists of the following:

- Assessing the age of your current workforce
- Studying the potential for attrition and retirement
- Giving consideration to vacancies that may be created by higher birth rates, an influx of immigrants into the community, or other economic factors
- Examining employee strength on the bench
- Installing grow-your-own-career ladders
- Looking for the best prospects in new places

The opposite approach to generational forecasting is called replacement planning. In this traditional recruitment method, a position opens up, the vacancy is advertised, interviews occur, and someone is hired. The risk is that an applicant may lack adequate knowledge or preparation to take on the role. In key jobs such as the principalship, premature promotions can spell D-I-S-A-S-T-E-R. Fallout might include low staff morale, a dip in student achievement, unhappy parents, a tarnished school reputation, and political or legal mistakes necessitating hours of repair by higher-ups (Lovely, 2004).

Unless a school district gets lucky, replacement planning is costly. Not only does it perpetuate the status quo, it also leads to higher-than-normal turnover and can cause vacancies to remain unfilled for prolonged periods. Generational forecasting, on the other hand, is an economical way to sidestep the experience gap on the horizon while slowing down the attrition that is draining the bucket. As 64 million Baby Boomers gear up for retirement, the 39 million Generation Xers lined up to replace them make a paltry succession pool. Efforts to identify future educational leaders need to begin now. School districts that rely on haphazard hiring practices are certain to be left behind.

START YOUR OWN FARM TEAM

Sending a personnel manager over to the college job fair in April to find five new special education teachers for the fall is a common recruitment practice in school systems. The problem here is that there are a hundred other districts at the job fair looking for exactly the same thing.

A better strategy is to start your own farm team through a paraeducator-to-teacher program. With 500,000 paraeducators nationwide, these second stringers represent a promising source of new teachers. High-quality programs help instructional aides overcome financial barriers and the absence of recent college experience. One incentive might be to provide salary advancement credit while participants attend in-house training that readies them for university admission. Such opportunities appeal to Baby Boomers, who have the most financial obligations and embrace the idea of moving up in their careers.

To get Veteran paraeducators invested, districts can provide study skills classes that assist them in passing college entrance exams. Swapping years of classroom experience for university credit is another enticement. Once student teaching begins, aides can be granted a leave of absence to guarantee a position to return to in the event they decide to postpone teaching or if vacancies are not yet available. What better way to serve up the job security and benefit protection Veterans so strongly covet?

Last, to pique the interest of a cash-strapped Generation Xer, consider offering a one-time monetary bonus for the completion of staff development or provide tuition reimbursement for coursework taken outside the workday. Age-friendly pathways into teaching break the "class ceiling" that keeps classified employees in low-paying jobs and limits their potential.

School districts have to look no further than their own backyard to build up strength on their bench.

WHO'S ON FIRST?

When it comes to grooming the next generation of principals, schools aren't doing as well as they should. Only 27 percent of districts in the United States have programs to prepare or support aspiring leaders (Institute for Educational Leadership, 2000). According to NASSP Executive Director Gerald Tirozzi, "Some of the bigger school districts have enough sense to grow their own. They're developing teachers from within; they're giving quality internships and those folks are moving through the ranks" (Bowser, 2001). But most districts simply roll the dice and hope to get lucky when principal vacancies occur.

Ready-fire-aim recruitment tactics make little sense when it's so widely known that high-caliber leaders are hard to come by. Additionally, the most capable applicants tend to gravitate to more desirable settings, leaving struggling schools high and dry. Employers are finding out the hard way that holding an administrative credential does not guarantee quality or interest in someone becoming a principal.

Although *every* state has an ample number of people with administrative credentials, *no* state has enough people with the knowledge, talent, or desire to lead schools to excellence:

Texas certified more than 7,000 school administrators in a four-year period—enough to replace every practicing principal in the Lone Star State. But a university relations specialist in the Dallas Independent School District reported that aspiring principals who went through traditional training programs (as opposed to Dallas's partnership program with the University of North Texas) only yielded about 20 percent of the excellent candidates the district was willing to hire (Fry, Bottoms, O'Neill, & Jacobson, 2004).

Georgia has 3,200 licensed administrators for 2,000 public schools. Yet, when a large southern district considered 35 applicants for a high school principal vacancy in 2003, not a single one met the their criteria or needs (Fry, Bottoms, O'Neill, & Hill, 2003).

California issues 2,000 to 3,500 administrative credentials annually. But only 38 percent of the licensees assume leadership roles in the state's schools (Orozco & Oliver, 2001).

Given the grim reality that the principal shortage is not actually a supply issue, every district must take deliberate steps to keep the well from running dry. Sadly, no other profession outside of educational leadership experiences such disinterest after trainees have completed their initial preparation.

Table 4.1, "Building Up the Principal's Bench," outlines a five-tiered formula to prepare an all-purpose team of would-be principals. Without identifying employees with high leadership potential and scaffolding their careers, districts will go to their bench only to find it empty.

Table 4.1   Building Up the Principal's Bench

1. **Single out high performers.** Instead of relying on the inconsistent pool of self-selected candidates, principals and central office scouts should search for quality candidates by talking to faculty with a good track record. People who demonstrate relational savvy and success in moving teams forward are asked to serve on committees and head up curriculum activities. This scaffold helps individuals discover their leadership potential and stimulates an interest in school administration.

2. **Create gateway assignments.** Once quality teacher leaders are identified, their principals should invite them to participate in gateway assignments such as the Teaching Assistant Principalship (TAP) or Teachers on Special Assignment (TOSA). Entry-level assignments create a well-marked pathway into the assistant principal role. Duties can be structured to broaden hands-on experience in program coordination, student discipline, parent interaction, and community outreach. It is imperative that gateway assignments are easy to get into and out of and fall under the watchful eye of an effective principal.

3. **Pursue certification from the inside out.** Unfortunately, university-based leadership programs remain virtually untouched by state and national accountability measures. To nudge colleges along, districts should actively pursue partnerships that meet their needs. The emergence of distance learning and alternative credentialing routes provides a golden opportunity to shop around. Classes can meet at the central office, integrate online learning with seat time, use instructors from inside and outside the district, offer discounted tuition, and deliver a curriculum that blends academic rigor with huge doses of reality.

4. **Get it right through quality internships**. Administrative internships have been described as vessels that are leaky, rudderless, or still in dry dock (Fry, Bottoms, & O'Neill, 2005). Quality internships require close supervision by role models with a proven track record. Learning occurs via trial and error in an actual school setting. Assignments must (a) be full-time; (b) link performance to leadership standards; (c) include time for daily reflection and evaluation between the intern and mentor; and (d) gradually increase responsibility to lead, rather than merely prescribe a continuum to follow.

5. **Make the assistant principal job matter.** Without depth and complexity in the assignment, assistant principals may be able to manage a school, but will struggle to lead it. Job responsibilities should mirror the principalship. Assistant principals must be expected to resolve faculty conflicts, analyze and use data, and facilitate the development of learning communities. If such elements are missing from the playbook, districts end up promoting people who are neither equipped nor ready to captain the team.

Preparing the next generation of principals requires more than lip service. Revamping "come one, come all" college enrollment practices is a perfect launch point since not everyone is cut out to be a principal. Accepting all who apply without measuring their potential only serves to delude participants. Furthermore, it leads to the false hope that just because someone stood in line waiting to be promoted, he or she deserves to move up to the Major League.

Another area in need of an overhaul is the ready-made curriculum doled out by most universities. Instead of reading an article about teacher supervision, wannabe leaders should be taught how to evaluate teachers who dislike them. Brainstorming ways to handle a controversy doesn't have the same authenticity as a professor conducting a simulation with future principals. Thrusting a microphone into a graduate student's face, the professor announces, "This is Channel 2 News reporting live outside Pleasant Hills High School where a teacher has just been accused of having a sexual relationship with a student. Oh, look, here comes the principal now. Ms. Smith, can we have a comment?"

If administrator training programs expect to hit a home run, principals-in-the-making need to spend ample time in the batting cages. Conversely, if prospective players are cooped up in the dugout watching the action from afar, the game is likely to be a shutout.

Although talent cannot be taught, teachers with the right stuff can be groomed to become successful leaders. Rarely do districts sit back and wait for teachers to apply. But when it comes to administrators, too many are complacent. The welcome news is that it is never too late to start tapping into your human potential and build up your bench.

To examine how effective your organization is in developing quality leaders, complete the inventory "Attracting and Retaining High-Quality Leaders" in Resource A. As strengths and shortcomings are noted, a feasible plan should be created to select and secure the next generation of principals.

ON YOUR MARK, GET SET, GO!

When looking for teachers, school districts tend to target the same conventional workforce that has dominated public education for decades. Recruitment ads tout starting salaries, retiree benefits, and success stories. Employee handbooks are full of boastful facts and figures. But, the composition of contemporary job seekers involves a mixture of values. When trolling for candidates, employers have to be in the right place at the right time with the right message. Showing a spectacular video at a job fair where there are no prospects in the demographics needed is akin to playing a Viagra commercial on VH1.

Finding high-caliber employees calls for a modernized hiring process. A thorough analysis of the marketing tools that cater to various age groups is essential. Typical Baby Boomer campaigns might focus on the size of the district, the type of students served, achievement data, and opportunities for salary advancement. Glossy brochures with fancy charts and nicely clad men and women are a Boomer draw.

Using prestige tactics to attract the quintessential Generation Xer, however, may not earn you a second glance. What is likely to interest an applicant from this hip crowd is a dialed-in Podcast showing the progressive learning environment, the infusion of technology into the curriculum, people having fun at work, and a choice of schools at which to hang their hats. For Millennial appeal, images might include teachers reviewing assessment data together, Veteran mentors working with newbies, a roommate finder or housing options, and a decent living wage. Without a recruitment renaissance to target each generational perspective, your candidate pool is certain to be shallow.

To spiff up the recruitment process, human resource departments should take a look at whether current staffing mechanisms build a generational bridge or just widen the gap. Schools aren't known for being particularly aggressive or flamboyant when it comes to marketing themselves. But, with four generations of savvy applicants out there, it may be time to add new twists to old turns. Looking for employees in the regular places or assuming "just because you advertised, they will come" won't produce the desired results. Luring applicants to your workplace will depend on several multiage attractions.

BE ALL THAT YOU CAN BE

When it comes to finding and keeping a sustainable mixture of new recruits, no institution has been better at reinventing itself than the U.S. Army. The point in sharing their story is not to take sides one way or another on the merits of joining the military, but instead to illustrate how a very traditional organization has been able to find its mark, get set, and go.

Attracting recruits to serve in the army was fairly easy before World War II. Responding to its focus on masculinity, patriotism, and pride, young men were banging down the door to fight in World War II. Slogans, such as "Uncle Sam Wants You," still carry tremendous meaning for Veterans. However, by the end of the Vietnam War, a negative flavor had engulfed the military. An all-volunteer army created a recruitment conundrum. Undeterred, the army bounced back by going after large numbers of enlistment-age Baby Boomers. In 1973, they introduced a new slogan, "Join the people who have joined the army," to portray a more congenial and permissive armed forces (Lancaster & Stillman, 2002).

When the first wave of self-sufficient Generation Xers came of age, the army recognized the need to recruit them differently. Zeroing in on their disillusionment, the campaign highlighted the structure, direction, and sense of family the army provided. Young men and women were implored to make something of themselves and "Be all that you can be." The slogan became so recognizable, it was named by *Advertising Age* as the second-best slogan of the twentieth century, after McDonald's "You deserve a break today" (Lancaster & Stillman, 2002, pp. 164–165).

After failing to meet recruitment quotas for three out of five years between 1995 and 2000, the army ratcheted up its efforts to speak to the second wave of Generation X. "The Power of One" became the new mantra aimed at young adults who, as individuals, strived to make a difference and acquire skills for life. Although Veterans rebuked the slogan because it shifted the emphasis away from loyalty and teamwork, the army wasn't recruiting Veterans anymore, so it really didn't matter.

Prolonged conflicts in Iraq and Afghanistan have left the army struggling once again to meet its recruitment goals. Recently, the deputy chief of staff for personnel told the Senate Armed Services Committee that keeping up the army's strength is its greatest strategic challenge. One controversial tactic granted under the auspices of No Child Left Behind allows recruiters access to high school campuses. Less polarizing strategies include cash bonuses for new recruits, increased college scholarships, raising the maximum enlistment age for reservists and the National Guard, allowing resident aliens to apply for citizenship, and selling Baby Boomer parents on the benefits of having their Millennials in the military.

Without a draft to press young people into service, the army has to assure prospects that the military makes for an honorable calling and fruitful career. To that end, the latest tagline announces, "There are many ways to be a soldier." The cultural pride of Latinos is also being targeted in key cities with slogans such as, "*Yo soy el Army*" (I am the Army). The army Web site boasts hundreds of opportunities for Millennial enlistees to find their strengths—ranging from computer work, to physician's assistant, to fixing helicopters. Since military service is a matter of choice, the objective is to emphasize options that promise active duty and reserve personnel there is an army job just right for them.

Tapping into the occupational interest of a 22-year-old college graduate takes a different approach than satisfying a 65-year-old retired scientist. To reach multiple generations, an organization's recruitment palette should consist of many shades and textures. The "Ten Ways to Outlook Your Competition" in Figure 4.1 blends the best practices from public and private industry to help school districts get ahead.

Figure 4.1   Ten Ways to Outlook Your Competition

1. **Woo me.** Every recruitment message must contain a persuasive statement of what a district has to offer aimed at the generation it hopes to attract. Messages need to speak to the values of prospective employees, not to the values of the district. A great "woo me" technique was used by the Chicago City Schools to boost up its substitute pool. First, the district located retirees and told them how much they were needed. Then, shuttle rides were provided to and from job sites to ensure work wasn't turned down because it was too far from public transportation (Lancaster & Stillman, 2002). Knowing the right value proposition to tap into retirees provides a rich source of labor for school districts.

2. **Send the right messenger.** Your district may have the best interview questions in the land, but if the wrong people are asking them, it may not matter. To avoid a time warp, generational rapport has to be established between recruiters and recruitees. Pay attention to who represents your district at career fairs, in the personnel office, and on promotional videos. Stodgy messengers attract stodgy applicants. In this day and age, schools need employees with plenty of spunk, not a bunch of stuffed shirts.

3. *Te queremos!* Grass-roots efforts offer a number of effective routes to draw underrepresented groups into education. Multilingual recruiters, radio and print ads in more than one language, and culturally mixed interview panels loudly proclaim, "Te Queremos!" (We want you!). Adult education classes in test prep or English language development can steer immigrants and minorities your way. Early outreach programs that expose middle and high school students to teaching as a profession have proved to be quite successful in inner-city schools. Finally, college fellowships that underwrite the tuition of hundreds of students are being offered in places such as North Carolina in exchange for a commitment to teach in the state for at least four years. The point is to dive for diversity wherever you can.

4. **Be ready to have the tables turned.** Veterans and Baby Boomers understand the meaning of professional attire, good manners, and deference to the power brokers who have the authority to say "you're hired." But it's becoming more and more common for weary Generation X or confident Millennials to cross-examine interviewers with quips such as "What grade level will I have?" "What kind of support are you going to give me?" and "Why should I come work for you?" In today's seller's market, interviewers need to arrive at interviews prepared to have the tables turned. Instead of being offended, keep the answers tucked inside your hip pocket.

5. **Listen up!** Some applicants are fabulous at interviewing, but couldn't teach their way out of a paper bag. Open-ended interview questions such as "What classroom management strategies do you use?" or "Describe your strengths and weaknesses" allow candidates to make up answers that sound good or are politically correct, even though experiences are not necessarily true or realistic. Traditional interview questions can be leading and may actually communicate the answers an interviewee thinks the interviewer wants to hear.

   So how can principals avoid being duped by a smooth talker? How do personnel managers ensure that a fantastic applicant who isn't very perky does not get overlooked? To snag the best and bypass the rest, more and more districts are turning to automated telephone prescreeners, online surveys, and behaviorally designed interview questions (see "Resource B: Snag the Best and Bypass the Rest").

Behaviorally based instruments adhere to the premise that past behavior is predictive of future success. Listening to how an applicant responds in different scenarios enables interviewers to assess intangibles such as empathy, judgment, and rapport drive. Such resources not only streamline the selection process, they also provide reliable, unbiased measurements of a teacher's attitudes and beliefs about working with children.

6. **Pay attention to your ratings.** Just because you were great five years ago doesn't mean you're still great today. Too many districts rely on past successes to keep applicants coming. A good way to check your pulse is to survey new hires and find out why they picked your district over another. For people who turn down job offers, ask why they declined. Although the truth can hurt like a good spanking, it may also provide a long overdue wake-up call. Be sure to keep in touch with teachers after they're hired, too. This gives you an ongoing read on the happy meter.

7. **Make it a family affair.** Millennials put their parents on a pedestal and consult with them often. Take advantage of this by making recruitment a family affair. Consider hosting career fairs whereby applicants are encouraged to bring along Mom and Dad to confer with recruiters. Schedule high school parent nights to explain college loan forgiveness programs and the financial perks available to those who enter teaching. Pass out brochures with well-dressed Baby Boomers standing next to their newly minted university grad exclaiming, "She's not just our daughter. She's a teacher." Older administrators, who were raised to pave their own way in life, will probably get heartburn over such coddling. Simply explain that sometimes you need to break the mold to preserve great traditions.

8. **Hop on the fast track.** In today's world of instant information and instant results, there is no time to dawdle when it comes to employee recruitment. Buttons and banners have replaced fliers and Sunday help wanted ads. Personnel offices moving at a snail's pace to screen applications, schedule interviews, or make job offers are being left in the dust. Commercially produced software enables districts to accept online applications, route candidates for interviews, distribute reference forms, and apply for fingerprint clearance within nanoseconds. People hunt for jobs around the clock, heightening the expectation for a quick response. When districts snooze, they lose.

9. **Go global.** The nice thing about technology is that access to resources is never more than a click away. The American Association for Employment in Education (www.aaee.org) has developed state and regional links to connect applicants with school districts. The U.S. Department of Education helped launch the National Teacher Recruitment Clearinghouse (www.recruiting teachers.org), which provides numerous tools to expand applicant pools, respond to changing demographics, and retain talented teachers. Teach for America (www.teachforamerica.org) sends recent college graduates from every academic major into needy areas to teach for two years. The idea is to create a large, diverse workforce and show young people that education is the foundation of democracy. Virtual firms, such as Monster.com, generate visibility and increase job traffic for any organization, anytime, anywhere. The best way to emerge from the dark ages is to go global.

10. **Be nice.** According to the ancient Japanese, the reputation of a thousand years may be determined by the conduct of a single hour. Newfangled recruitment mechanisms won't mean much if people forget to be nice. Don't let all the gadgetry disguise how staff members treat applicants. Indifference or poor attitudes of current employees will drive prospective employees away in a New York minute. To remain on the cutting edge, make sure the human touch is not overshadowed by automated or faceless communication.

HANDLE WITH CARE

Within each school community, there is a distinct culture that prescribes "the way we do things around here" (Deal & Peterson, 1999). The manner in which new recruits are assimilated into a school, for example, speaks volumes about its culture. Conventional beliefs about seniority usually dictate how far the welcome mat is rolled out.

Regrettably, a common initiation for younger staff members is the ritual of "hazing." Hazing involves customary practices that result in beginning teachers experiencing poorer working conditions than their older counterparts (Patterson, 2004). Assigning the least experienced teachers to the neediest students, giving combination classes or new courses to the last hired, or remanding rookies to classrooms far away from colleagues places them in an untenable situation.

Almost as bad as hazing is the similar practice of poaching. Poaching occurs when a vacated classroom is raided of materials and furniture so that when a newcomer steps in, he or she is left with broken desks, inadequate supplies, and lots of useless junk. These sanctioned acts, which target beginning teachers, lead to frustration, fatigue, and failure.

With all the known dangers of hazing and poaching, why is such harmful adult behavior still tolerated inside the schoolhouse? Although the outcome may not rise to the level of severity as witnessed on fraternity row or the great plains of Africa, the casualties often end up just as emotionally scarred. Table 4.2, the "Hazed and Confused" storyboard illustrates how young victims are affected by this mistreatment.

Addressing variances between seasoned faculty and novices requires purging the outdated practices that drive Generation X from the profession and discourage Millennials from signing on in the first place. It's not a matter of treating new teachers differently, it's a matter of treating them right. Seniority-based traditions damage a new teacher's psyche and hinder the school's ability to retain them. The following actions will help site leaders challenge these practices and even the score:

- **Hire new staff as early as possible.** Waiting to hire teachers until the last minute or after the school year is underway forces newcomers to be stuck with the leftovers.

- **Offer first-timers a survivable experience.** Assign beginning teachers to their own classroom; don't ask them to teach more than two preps; limit extra duties, club sponsorships, and cocurricular activities; and provide a balance of low- and high-level students/course loads.

Table 4.2   Storyboard: Hazed and Confused

Jason's Junket	Claire's Catastrophe
After finishing my degree at Columbia University, I was elated for the chance to work with needy students in a beleaguered community in upstate New York. Within months, however, I was a beaten-down newcomer among an unwelcoming staff. Many of my coworkers found little joy in their job, having been enmeshed in a history of discord between the central office and the union. Morale never seemed to bounce back after a strike several years earlier. Compounding matters, the town's population had shifted from middle-class industrial workers to immigrants and welfare cases. *Some of the faculty openly admitted that they continued teaching simply because they "had to pay the rent." The only heroes on staff were antiheroic. As one of the few young teachers, I quickly became isolated and had no one to share my frustrations with.* Jason Teller now teaches at a suburban high school.	*Instead of embracing new people for choosing such a noble profession and congratulating them for taking this first step, it's like, "Oh you're new. You have no seniority. You get no favors or perks. But here's a cart and some bungee cords to haul your stuff around as you travel each period from one end of the campus to the other."* *Teaching three different preps with leftover materials from the 30-year Veteran I replaced isn't my idea of a good time. I've lost a lot of friends at this school because of what seem to be nitpicky things that are all a really big deal.* Claire Lopez left teaching after five years to sell real estate.

• **Start a neighborhood watch.** To combat isolation, place novices near helpful department- or grade-level Veterans. Explain to the older residents that you are counting on them to look out for their neighbors. Remind staff that it really does take a village to raise a new teacher.

• **Provide the core essentials.** The minute a new hire shows up on your doorstep, he or she should receive a faculty handbook and resource binder containing school policies, content standards, course outlines, assessment and grading criteria, and so forth.

• **Give newcomers adequate textbooks, equipment, and supplies.** Forcing rookies to scavenge around for basic materials is demeaning and frustrating. If for some reason teacher's editions, student texts, or other resources are on back order, ask senior teachers to give up their materials temporarily until the items arrive.

- **Orient new staff to the campus.** Don't wait until the first fire drill to explain where students are supposed to line up. Avoid engaging newcomers in a game of hide-and-seek as they search for P.E. equipment, the science cart, or math manipulatives. This is a waste of precious time.

- **Conduct weekly checkups.** Make it your mission at least once a week to ask every new teacher on your campus, "How are you doing?" "What do you need?" "In what ways are your colleagues helping you?" This provides firsthand information about the well-being of younger staff rather than relying on others to tell you about problems, or worse, assuming no news is good news.

There is no doubt that Generation X and Millennials yearn for a sense of belonging and inclusion in the workplace, but not in the same benign way as Veterans or Baby Boomers. To Generation X, it means having an egalitarian, not a hierarchical, relationship with coworkers and supervisors. To a Millennial, it means having people to confide in and being able to talk to a boss about progress.

Unlike other cohorts, Millennials actually look to older colleagues as a resource. The worst thing a school can do is stick brand-new teachers in the closet and expect them to fend for themselves. Dismissing the generational wiring of first- and second-year teachers will make it tough to hold onto them. After all, beginners are fragile and must be handled with care.

CONCLUSION: BECOME FIRST-RATE

Good employees don't grow on trees. In an hourglass society, applicants can be choosy. Licensing reciprocity between states and the portability of experience credit makes it easier for senior teachers to relocate, too. While job-hopping for Veterans and Baby Boomers carried a stigma and occurred only if necessary, job-hopping for Generation X is considered essential for advancement. For Millennials, job-hopping is predicted to become routine. Although Millennials place greater value on loyalty than Generation X, the need to be busy and stimulated will propel them to have multiple careers. Teaching high school by day, attending college at night, and selling real estate on the weekends, Millennials have the perseverance and panache to be masters of it all.

Employee recruitment is a complex, multilayered function. Districts that fervently hold onto the recruitment methods that were satisfactory a decade or two ago will find themselves at a disadvantage. While the experience of seasoned staff is leveraged, the enthusiasm of novices can be bottled. Convincing parents that teaching is the epicenter of all professions should be an integral part of this recruitment renaissance. Mom's and Dad's opinions and counsel have a huge influence on a Millennial's career decisions.

With the Internet opening doors 24/7, districts are foolish not to rely on technology as a primary resource for attracting young, old, and in-betweens. To be a first-rate employer, you have to hire first-rate people. But, if your organization is satisfied being second-rate, you'll be lucky to hire third-rate people. Filling your succession pool with first-rate people means making sure your human potential is ageless.

Creating Synergy in the Schoolhouse

The administrator who can get the maximum effort out of everyone in the organization is always a cut above the rest.

—Robert Ramsey

Just beneath the surface of everyday life in a school is a cascade of thought and activity that determines how people act, what they talk about, how they function as a group, what they wear, how they treat students, what they say about parents, and how they view their jobs. This aura captures the essence of an organization and is referred to as simply "The Culture." Strong cultures have powerful effects on the passion, purpose, and productivity embodying a workplace. Weak cultures have the same effect, but in reverse. Without looking at the generational trademarks that nudge the personality of a school in one direction or another, it is impossible to spawn greater alignment.

As noted in Chapter 3, *communication* is the action verb of generational leadership. Culture builders use stories and persuasion to unlock doorways that have long been dead-bolted shut. Whether linking with the past, reinvigorating the present, or outlining a more promising future, conversations must include multiple perspectives. Although Baby Boomers and Generation X comprise the bulk of today's workforce, Veterans and Millennials can't be carved out of the equation (see Table 5.1, "The

Table 5.1   The Graying Workforce

Age Group	Percentage of Workforce in 2002	Percentage of Workforce in 2012	Percentage of
Over 65	3.1%	3.9%	0.8%
40–64	50.0%	52.9%	2.9%
25–39	34.6%	31.8%	−2.8%
16–24	15.7%	15.0%	−.7%

SOURCE: U.S. Bureau of Labor Statistics.

Graying Workforce"). Since there is no blueprint on exactly how to get the maximum effort out of employees, the rule of thumb is to customize your own solutions, with modest help from the outside.

THE DEMOGRAPHIC GULCH

As the quest to maintain synergy inside the schoolhouse accelerates, keep in mind that employees bring their own motivation with them to work. Tapping into this motivation means unleashing individual talent, rather than restraining people by rule, policy, or coercion. Once the last of the Boomer superintendents exit the stage in ten years, American schools will be a completely Generation X– and Millennial-led environment, serving a new generation of elementary children (Strauss, 2005). Although the gap may narrow slightly, rifts over work ethics and priorities are likely to remain an issue. School systems have to level the playing field in order to perpetuate a stronger sense of affiliation throughout every corridor.

Multiage programming calls for a change in interplay between district governance and the management of employees. Here's why: A Veteran trustee, baffled that teachers aren't satisfied with a 2 percent raise, is only going to be further annoyed when the Generation X union president refers to the school board as "clueless" and admonishes trustees for thinking teachers are about to work for free. A Boomer maintenance director who tells a new custodian he should "be grateful just to have a job" may find himself in a pickle when the Millennial turns in his keys and accepts an offer in the neighboring district.

Brushing aside the mental models of Generation X or Millennials as a phase deludes older supervisors and digs a deeper demographic gulch. Younger employees won't grow out of these attitudes, nor is there a harder working, more conciliatory labor force waiting around the corner. Using the wrong generational template hastens a situation to go sideways and makes recovery difficult (see Table 5.2, "When Things Go Sideways"). On the other hand, taking time to understand what pushes someone's buttons enables a manager to temper his or her comments and avoid age-induced grudges.

Teachers and administrators quit their jobs when they are unhappy or feel no one in the organization cares about them. Since there are plenty of

Table 5.2   When Things Go Sideways

	Pet Peeves	Gaffes That Cause Grudges
For Veterans	✓ Profanity and bad grammar ✓ Indiscretion ✓ Disorganization ✓ Lack of respect for traditions ✓ Disregard for experience	✓ "We really don't have a plan. Let's just wing it." ✓ "Tell me again when you said you were retiring." ✓ "Can't you do that any faster?" ✓ "Whaaazzzup dude?"
For Baby Boomers	✓ Unfriendliness ✓ Slackers ✓ Challenges to their authority ✓ Political incorrectness	✓ "This teamwork thing stinks." ✓ "I'm too busy to come to your meeting." ✓ "Do you even know how to turn on your computer?" ✓ "Whatever!"
For Generation X	✓ Schmoozing ✓ Stern lectures ✓ Clichés, acronyms, jargon ✓ Too many rules and policies ✓ Inefficiency	✓ "If you cared about the team, you'd stay late like the rest of us." ✓ "We have to do this because the district office said so." ✓ "You need to earn your stripes before getting that assignment." ✓ "Didn't you read it in the policy manual?"
For Millennials	✓ Cynicism and negativity ✓ Unfair treatment ✓ Sarcasm ✓ Condescending remarks ✓ Low expectations	✓ "You probably don't have anything to add since you're new." ✓ "Are you sure you aren't supposed to be *in* high school instead of teaching it?" ✓ "You ought to be happy just to have a job." ✓ "When I was your age . . ."

other employment options available, there's no need to stick around a school and be miserable. Recognizing contributions, building rapport, and providing a smorgasbord of learning opportunities breed loyalty. Even if a district is able to develop a large percentage of its workforce from within, figuring out how to hold onto people is critically important, too. When an institution shows that it values employees, there is a strong desire to be affiliated with it. On the other hand, if assignments lack stimulation, relationships are lousy, or staff members feel they are not making a difference, the institution will nosedive toward mediocrity.

HI HO, HI HO, iT'S OFF TO WORK WE GO

Several companies throughout the United States have made headlines in establishing harmonious and growth-oriented work environments. Although skeptics might decry that private enterprise isn't in the delicate business of educating children, optimists (Boomers, most likely) would counter that we can all learn from one another. From Starbucks to Ben & Jerry's to 24 Hour Fitness, corporate America is doing remarkably well in creating age-friendly workplaces. Through an emphasis on flexibility, respect, appreciation for differences, an expansive talent pool, and top-notch service, these standouts know how to energize and empower their people.

Becoming a great place to work is about more than coffee, ice cream, or the elliptical trainer. At Starbucks, for example, the perfect blend of products and people is brewed by making every employee a "partner." From stock options to individualized benefit plans, partners recognize that the company's success depends on their success. The rich employee base percolates from dignity, diversity, and respect as job seekers line up in droves to be part of this team. Try to catch the esprit de corps in action on your next visit to Starbucks. While baristas rally and adjust to keep up with customer demands, watch how each frappuccino and double latte is dispersed with pleasant efficiency.

Ice cream phenomenon Ben & Jerry's scoops out its corporate utopia by creating recognition that comes in a variety of flavors. In an ambience of informality, hard work is balanced with meaningful rewards. A special force known as the Joy Gang consults with staff to create workplace diversions (Zemke, Raines, & Filipczak, 2000). This social committee isn't about making fun obligatory. Rather, time is spent researching the incentives and events that mean the most to people. Whether it's bringing in massage therapists to relieve tension, dress-up days, letting pooches tag along to work, or rocking out at the annual music festival, the Joy Gang hits its mark through individualized inspiration. The point is that when people are working 70 hours a week, they ought to have a barrel of fun doing it. At Ben & Jerry's, wholesome ingredients are used to concoct every reward and celebration. And when a recipe isn't working, it is duly laid to rest in the graveyard with all the other dearly departed flavors.

Health club extraordinaire 24 Hour Fitness is pumping up its customer base through spacious facilities, affordable fees, and ease of use. But the biggest draw is that people can work out any time—day or night. And where there are fitness fanatics, there are employees. Imagine being able to say to your boss, "I'll take the 10:00 p.m. to 4:00 a.m. shift, please." Flexible work schedules are a generational gold mine. Although children don't attend school at midnight, zero periods, year-round calendars, summer sessions, virtual learning, and weekend study clubs provide job options beyond the traditional school day.

In generationally friendly workplaces, the corporate brass is keenly aware that happy employees make for happy customers. And happy customers parlay into higher profits. The same is true in schools. Happy teachers perpetuate happy students. Happy students outperform their unhappy peers. And if students are happy, parents are delighted. Happy parents, in turn, love to brag about their neighborhood school. As the school's good reputation spreads, applicants flock there from far and wide. And so the life cycle continues in creating and sustaining exceptional places to work.

THE SYNERGY DOCTRINE

If employees are the heart and soul of an organization, demographic time clocks must be synchronized to engage and inspire them. Creating synergy in the schoolhouse begins by replacing the Golden Rule, Do unto others as you would have others do unto you, with the Titanium Rule, Do unto others, keeping their generational preference in mind (Raines, 2003, p. 34). The Golden Rule assumes everyone is motivated exactly as you are. In essence, if you thrive on competition, then teachers get an adrenaline rush from it, too. If you enjoy public praise, then your secretary must surely revel in it.

Obviously, we don't all breathe the same psychological oxygen. Without respect for divergent thinking, the sum of a district's parts will never equal more than its whole. The best leaders promote synergy by rejecting the Golden Rule and deciding instead what makes each person tick. Management by exception elevates employee engagement to new heights.

The synergy doctrine erases cross-age boundaries that impede collaboration and paves the way for designing age-friendly school systems. Improving the quality of public education from the inside out requires those in charge to model, organize, protect, and reward the things that matter most. Synergy spawns momentum; momentum improves performance.

The seven dimensions that follow form the building blocks in satisfying a mixed workforce and stimulating "above and beyond" behavior:

Seize your assets

Yield to diversity

Nurture retention

Exercise flexibility

Recognize and reward

Galvanize learning

Yin-and-yang leadership

1. **Seize your assets:** Effective leaders don't try to make boring jobs or boring people interesting. Instead, they seize their assets by preventing interesting people and interesting jobs from becoming dull. Risks are encouraged and mistakes minimized to keep the work environment vibrant and innovative. Everyone from the custodian, to the mailroom clerk, to the almost-ready-to-retire teacher is treated as if he or she has something remarkable to offer. Expecting the best of each staff member, including yourself, is a two-for-one deal. Employees feel valued and value their employer in return. If people are the problem in your school, then you need to look at them as the solution, too.

2. **Yield to diversity:** It is natural to want to hire individuals who look and act just like you. However, carbon copy selection is unhealthy for schools and causes stagnation. When everyone agrees all the time or when people are afraid to rattle the cages, learning either plateaus or plummets. Since schools are a microcosm of society, those who work in them have to identify with a wide range of intellectual, political, cultural, ethnic, and social forces. Districts inundated with sameness end up with variations of the same. Yield to diversity by hiring people who think and sound differently than you.

3. **Nurture retention:** Hasty hiring decisions often result in mismatched employees and bad chemistry. Hence, the ideal way to

nurture retention is to hire for fit and train for skill. It's easy to teach teachers about content standards and grading criteria. But it's next to impossible to teach them how to be compassionate and nice. Capitalize on what individuals do well instead of scrutinizing what they do poorly. Expecting a faculty to bend to the "my way or the highway" mentality is onerous and outdated. Rather than trying to change someone, school leaders are far better served putting employees in situations where their strengths stand out and their flaws are barely noticed.

4. **Exercise flexibility:** Letting teachers work part-time, approving principal job shares, permitting special education staff to complete paperwork at home, or encouraging bus drivers to bid on a 4/10 workweek are all examples of how to "flexercise" in the schoolhouse. Although it can be complex juggling a Monday-Wednesday-Friday routine, the payoffs are worth it.

   At a time when schools have limited dollars to spend, alternate schedules are a real coup in winning over employees. Young and old alike are more anxious than ever before to balance career, family, and outside interests. Flexercising is a way for public education to catch up with the corporate world in offering a menu of age-friendly work options (See Figure 5.1, "Flexercise Work Schedules").

5. **Recognize and reward:** The effects of recognition in the workplace have been substantiated by a century of research. The key is to figure out what motivates each employee and determine how folks like their accolades served up. For a Veteran, it may be a classroom close to the office. For a Baby Boomer, it might be a personal parking space. For a Generation Xer, perhaps it's an e-mail from the principal saying, "Thanks for being on duty in the hallway today." And for a Millennial, it could be a "Hip Hip Hooray" certificate given in front of peers to acknowledge contributions on a team project.

   Public and private praise has many purposes beyond simple courtesy. To a teacher, it signifies an administrator noticed and cared. To the rest of the school, it elevates role models and communicates the standards that constitute great performance. Tailoring incentives to age-driven preferences is a low-cost investment that yields big dividends in the end. It's the attention, not the reward itself, that matters most to people (See Figure 5.2, "Tickle My Fancy").

Figure 5.1   Flexercise Work Schedules

Flex Time

- Individualized start/end times that remain constant each day
- Individualized start/end times that vary each day
- Individualized start/end times with changing daily hours
- Extended lunch times offset by additional hours at the beginning/end of the day

Compressed Workweek

- A full workweek that is less than five days; or
- Two full-time workweeks compressed into 9- or 9½-hour days

Job Sharing/Partnerships

- Two staff members sharing one full-time position
- Responsibilities split evenly or unevenly, depending on what's mutually agreed upon by partners and the supervisor (see Resource C for sample teacher contract)

Reduced Hours/Part-Time

- Decreasing hours worked to less than a full-time position

Telecommuting

- Fulfilling a portion of job responsibilities offsite using computers, cell phones, and other electronic devices
- Supervisor and staff member agree whether telecommuting is done for a set number of hours each week or for a specified period of time

Homesourcing

- Allow employees to work completely from home
- Monthly or bimonthly training at the central office to learn new skills and be brought up to speed on what's happening in the organization

---

6. **Galvanize learning:** Generationally savvy schools set aside time for faculty to reflect on instructional practices, refine skills, and build knowledge. Professional development is embedded into the context of the workday, so it is not seen as giving teachers more to do. A long-term commitment is bolstered as staff members learn and grow in ways adapted to their own particular style.

   Veterans respond to training supported by logic and research. They learn best in traditional classroom settings with presenters who look and act professional. Conversely, Baby Boomers prefer varied learning formats that encourage them to deepen relationships with colleagues. They strive to understand how a particular topic will catapult them ahead or make them better than they already are.

Figure 5.2   Tickle My Fancy

If you think it takes big bucks to win over employees, think again. Although studies confirm that today's workers expect to receive competitive benefits and wages, it is not the primary reason they join or stay with an organization. The following motivators are listed in priority order:

1. Support and involvement (information from my boss, inclusion in decisions, acceptance of mistakes)

2. Personal praise

3. Autonomy and authority (getting to decide how work is done, choice of assignments)

4. Flexible working hours

5. Learning and development

6. Time with my manager

7. Written praise

8. Electronic praise

9. Public praise

10. Cash incentives (small cash awards, stipends, gift certificates)

11. Achievement awards (years of service, special certificates, employee of the month)

12. Nominal gifts/food (flowers, mementos, lunch on the boss, office treats)

13. Public perks (special privileges, parking space, pass-around trophy)

SOURCE: From Nelson, B., *1001 Ways to Reward Employees* and *The 1001 Rewards & Recognition Fieldbook*. Reprinted with permission.

Generation X enjoys self-directed activities that move along briskly. This less patient cohort resents being held hostage in a three-day seminar that could easily have been condensed to a day. Conversely, Millennials live for training that incorporates peer interaction, especially when older mentors are involved. Since they started learning in the womb, there is a universal expectation that employers will provide plenty of opportunities to gain knowledge and reduce work-related stress. Like Generation X, Millennials lose interest quickly, so training should be interactive and engaging.

Before calling class to order, think about how you might reach out and touch an intergenerational audience. Table 5.3, "Training Template: Meeting the Needs of a Mixed Crowd," outlines the manner in which each generation learns best.

Table 5.3 Training Template: Meeting the Needs of a Mixed Crowd

Participant	Class Setting	Style of Presenter	Substance	Worries and Aversions
Veteran	✓ Traditional classroom environment ✓ Stress free; unhurried ✓ Opportunity to practice skills privately ✓ Adequate breaks	✓ Unemotional and logical ✓ Credible experiences ✓ Older, more mature presenters who speak the same language ✓ Coaches in a tactful way	✓ Large print materials ✓ Reader's Digest facts and summaries ✓ Actual examples ✓ Minimal techno-bells and -whistles	✓ Being called on and not knowing the answer ✓ Stories that are too personal ✓ Overly technical information ✓ Coddling younger participants ✓ Rudeness
Baby Boomer	✓ Organized for group interaction ✓ Chance to network ✓ Open-ended discussions ✓ Participation in setting the agenda	✓ Recognizes them for what they already know ✓ Comes across as a friendly equal (never call them ma'am or sir) ✓ Uses personal examples	✓ Easy to scan ✓ Well organized ✓ Icebreakers; team-building exercises ✓ Case studies	✓ Looking foolish in front of peers (nix the role-play) ✓ Content that doesn't apply to their current assignment ✓ All the work piling up back at school or the office
Generation X	✓ Structured so they can work at own pace ✓ Distance learning and independent study ✓ On-the-job training	✓ Gets right to the point ✓ Informal and fun loving ✓ Earns their respect ✓ Doesn't hover over them ✓ Gives lots of feedback	✓ Bulleted to highlight key points ✓ Headlines and lists ✓ Role-play (unfazed about looking clumsy)	✓ Reteaching them what they already know ✓ Beating a topic to death ✓ Using overheads ✓ Boredom
Millennial	✓ Versatile ✓ Combines teamwork with technology ✓ Ability to get up and move around the room when tasks are finished	✓ Positive and upbeat ✓ Makes purpose, process, and payoffs clear ✓ Listens; validates ideas ✓ Recognizes them as lifelong learners	✓ Retooling what they know to adapt to workplace changes ✓ Music, art, and games ✓ Ideas for dealing with difficult parents	✓ Moving too slowly ✓ Lecturing ✓ Out-of-date technology ✓ Implying they can't do something ✓ Criticism

7. **Yin-and-yang leadership:** Effective leaders behave with certain finesse, yet are direct and clear about what is expected of employees. They know how and when to make exceptions without being accused of favoritism or causing a faculty revolt. Balancing a concern for task attainment with a concern for people, these yin-and-yang masters decide when to teach and when to learn, when to fix and when to nix. Some days you'll find them pushing the wagon along and other days you'll see them pulling it. Excellence is a habit, not a fleeting event. Through an individualized, fluid style, successful bosses can get a team to follow them to the moon.

Common sense tells us that loyalty isn't bought with a paycheck. Unfortunately, common sense doesn't always parlay into common practice in schools. It's not what board members, superintendents, principals, or central office staff say that counts most with employees. It's what they do. Managers who try to mandate collegiality or attempt to improve job satisfaction through edict or policy are spinning their wheels. Without the synergy doctrine to heighten cross-age engagement, school leaders can expect a lackluster response to new initiatives, programs, or reforms.

DIPLOMACY: NEW WORD OF THE DAY

If you're a Veteran, you might be reading this chapter thinking, "Whatever happened to people just being grateful to have a job?" Driven Baby Boomers are pondering, "If I'm working 12 hours a day, is it really fair that another principal gets to stay home on Friday?" Doubtful Generation X is already compiling a list of reasons why these ideas won't work in their district: union contracts, education codes, community expectations, bell schedules, and an uptight school board.

Rest assured. These principles are easily adaptable in schools if you are willing to pursue a different perspective. In fact, former Secretary of State Colin Powell demonstrated that even big government is able to honor employees in age-sensitive ways. Powell raised eyebrows on occasion when he brought junior staffers into the Oval Office to brief the President. On other occasions he would write compliments on communiqués written by midlevel state department officials.

An acquaintance who works in the foreign service told us another amazing story about Secretary Powell. After the tsunami smashed ashore on December 26, 2004, she was dispatched from her post in Kuala Lumpur to Bangkok to assist in tracking down missing Americans.

Her counterparts from the Bangkok embassy were sent to Phuket for the grim task of recovering bodies.

As the senior ranking embassy official at the time, our friend was assigned to meet Secretary Powell and Governor Jeb Bush, who headed the American delegation. Despite supervising employees who worked thousands of miles from the corporate office, Powell had an uncanny ability to make people feel connected. No matter what minor incident or major disaster the secretary handled, he always let staff know how pivotal they were to the operation's success.

When the secretary encountered our friend in Thailand, he expressed his gratitude for the assistance she had personally offered in the recovery efforts. Even though he was in the final weeks of his job, Powell never wavered in his commitment to let employees know they made a difference. If muckety-mucks in the White House can take the time to pay more attention to their people, then muckety-mucks in the schoolhouse can, too.

Managing and motivating a generational mix requires a new word of the day: *diplomacy*. Role models such as Colin Powell deal with the world as it is in order to make it more of what they would like it to be. Genuine diplomacy is the combination of power and persuasion, the orchestration of words and deeds in the pursuit of objectives (Powell, 2004). Powell says if you want to endure without resorting to force, you must be patient and wise in the face of danger and bold and strong in the face of opportunity.

If reducing teacher turnover or improving employee morale is a goal in your organization, then look no further than the principal's office. Although sad but true, a major reason teachers transfer or leave the profession is due to a lack of support from their principal. A teacher from Fairfax County, Virginia, hit the nail on the head when she said, "Principals set up an environment that either makes you want to strive to be better at what you do or makes you want to run from what you do" (Gordon, 2004 March).

Great principals rely on their moral compass to navigate pressures from above, below, and in between. They study the attitudes that pose a barrier to action, take notice of age-driven styles, and emphasize problems that unite people, instead of fixating on problems that divide them. Not a single teacher is permitted to linger on the sidelines while others tend to the troubled youth or worry about the failure rate. Every team member is positioned at center court with a 360-degree view of the action.

No one has studied principal talent more than the Gallup Organization. Through an in-depth examination of principals across North America, Gallup has isolated the genetic coding that distinguishes top contenders from average ones. "The Diplomacy Code" in the sidebar

The Diplomacy Code

Principals with the highest ratings of effectiveness from supervisors and teachers bring diplomatic talents to the assignment, which include the following characteristics:

Motivators

- **Vision:** Communicate a picture of what the school can become.
- **Internal motivation:** Possess a strong work ethic, goal orientation, and an innate drive to succeed.
- **External motivation:** Claim big goals for the school and move people forward in achieving them.

Relationship Builders

- **Relator:** Create friendships.
- **Feelings:** Become highly attuned to the feelings of others.
- **Growing others:** Help staff grow professionally; find opportunities for people to do new things.
- **Ownership:** Personally own what happens in the school.

Agents of Change

- **Team:** Gain commitment from individuals to work as a group.
- **Positivity:** Bounce back from setbacks; hopeful and resilient.
- **Stimulator:** Create excitement, fun, and joy within the school.
- **Arranger:** Provide for teachers' needs.
- **Action oriented:** Push for action and improvement.

SOURCE: From Gordon, G., *Replacing a Generation of School Leaders*, copyright © 2005, The Gallup Organization. Reprinted with permission.

NOTE: For more information on Gallup's Leadership Development Program, contact Gary Evans at 402-938-6517 or visit the Education Division Web site at http://education.gallup.com.

highlights the defining characteristics of principals who relate to all perspectives, reframe conversations from what cannot be done to what can, and broker deals to bring harmony to the workplace. Greatness lies not in where these principals stand, but in which direction they are moving their school.

Great principals are ambassadors of learning by either (a) hiring better teachers or (b) improving those they have. The standouts know when it is necessary to deviate from the norm or use unorthodox measures to get an employee to push the envelope. Seeing the job as a calling, they stick with it irrespective of obstacles or setbacks. Great principals have indeed cracked the code for intergenerational leadership: *There is no such thing as diplomatic immunity inside the principal's office.*

CONNECTING THE DOTS

Administrators and teachers are busy people. Finding time to join forces is hampered by the rigid nature of school calendars, master schedules, the layout of the facility, and past practice. For nearly a century, things such as academic freedom and redundancy have remained closely guarded traditions. Even though Johnny may have read *Huckleberry Finn* three times, he didn't read it with Ms. Wonderful who has a kinship with Mark Twain that convinces her she can make the novel seem different.

As shared in Chapter 3, a degree of adult dysfunction and denial is tolerated in schools primarily because educators have yet to master the art of working together. Without the right leadership to broker collaboration, indifference or isolation are bound to prevail.

Each generation embraces its own approach to career development, job expectations, money, and rewards. Variances depend upon what was ingrained during the formative years of childhood. For example, Veterans and Baby Boomers were taught that a decent day's work earned you a decent day's pay. Devotion to a job often came at the expense of family and friends. Generation X watched how this all-consuming work ethic took a toll on Mom and Dad's marriage, health, and overall well-being. As a result, they have vowed not to repeat the mistakes of their elders. To younger generations, productivity and long hours are not part and parcel of a good life.

Not all schoolhouse occupants will see eye to eye no matter whether they inhabit the same generational bungalow or reside a generational neighborhood apart. How, then, should teachers be guided in relating to the disparate ages of constituents and coworkers? For starters, the "Synergy Audit" in Resource D can be used to assess the ebb and flow of happiness in your current work setting. Once the audit is complete, identify a focus point where you can begin promoting a more demographically friendly environment. Never lose sight of the fact that being sensitive and patient has nothing to do with age.

School leaders have to work a lot harder than they did 10 or 15 years ago to connect the dots. These words of wisdom can help fuse the four generational personalities into the character of a school or district and keep your workplace out of the gulch:

1. **If new to a position, seek out others who have been around the block**. Guidance and support from "matures" can prove invaluable. Seasoned employees know the location of land mines and are familiar with ways around them.

2. **Let people argue with you, even if they're a lot younger.** Open your door and encourage staff to come in with their opinions or arguments. Even if an idea seems far-fetched, it is good to know where younger employees stand.

3. **Don't paint every generation with the same brush.** Over-generalizations lead to faulty assumptions. Faulty assumptions perpetuate biases that are hard to erase down the road.

4. **Wait your turn.** Ascending to a position of power too quickly may place you in a situation beyond your present handling capacity. Temper your exuberance by studying the cultural landscape and learning from those who are held in high regard.

5. **Be wise with words.** Exercise care when speaking or writing about anything that has a sweeping impact on the workplace. It is difficult, if not impossible, for a leader to recover from a slip of the tongue or a slip of the keyboard.

6. **In any crisis, stop and step away from the confusion.** Ask yourself two simple questions: What am I doing that I shouldn't be doing? What am I not doing that I ought to be doing to influence the situation in our favor? Work actively to shape the crisis and create success (Powell, 2004).

7. **Swallow your pride.** It's easy to be blinded by past success, especially if you've been around awhile. When criticism surfaces, listen rather than get defensive. If criticism is unwarranted, it will be revealed over time. If criticism is deserved, admit your mistakes and move on.

CONCLUSION: NOT TOO YOUNG, NOT TOO OLD

It's a fact: Employees are happier and more productive when jobs are challenging and they feel appreciated. People contribute to the betterment of the organization if rewards are valued and tied to specific outcomes. Teachers actually become more effective when they respect and rely on the talents of colleagues to reach students. Principals elevate their effectiveness by respecting and relying on the talents of their teachers. Superintendents and school boards continue this reciprocal process through shared values and a common vision. In this atmosphere, the collective wisdom of the team replaces any need for individual victory, no matter where you happen to be in the hierarchy.

History has taught us that when an enterprise is too young or too old, it can run aground. Take the downfall of Enron as a case in point (Wendover & Garciulo, 2006). With most managers and employees in their twenties, there was a lot of living on the edge. Yet, as a group, these corporate zealots lacked the maturity to make sound business decisions. Inexperience prompted key policymakers to pursue ill-advised and risky financial endeavors, ultimately leading to the company's demise. With age comes deliberation that prevents costly errors down the road.

On the other hand, we have witnessed vintage thinkers being trounced by upstarts who apply fresh ideas to solve age-old problems. Look at how Dell Computers zipped past IBM by focusing on issues such as faster delivery time, reduced operational costs, and better customer service. Being overly cautious or underestimating market demands can put you out of business, too. If all innovations are ignored to retain the comforts of what is familiar, schools will become stuck in the past.

To get the temperature just right in your workplace, younger administrators must understand the experiences that drive the desires and decisions of older staff. On the other hand, mature leaders need to strike a balance between using the past as a yardstick and catapulting too far into the future. If you supervise Generation X or Millennial employees, dismissing their ideas on the basis of inexperience will create a demographic rift that is hard to bridge. If you supervise Veterans or Baby Boomers, rolling your eyes at the drabness of their traditions may place you in the middle of a silent coup.

School leaders manage people ranging in age from their early twenties to their mid-sixties, and even beyond. Integrating differences in attitude and experience is paramount for success. Conflict between younger and older employees usually boils down to poor communication. Poor communication limits understanding and ultimately stalls progress. And a lack of progress eventually leads to decay.

Pay attention to how employees react to the temperature inside the schoolhouse and adjust the thermostat accordingly. Creating a comfortable, inviting climate encourages faculty members to grow into a symbiotic team where age doesn't matter.

Here Come the Millennials, Ready or Not!

Our generation isn't all about sex, drugs, and violence. It's about technology, discovery, and coming together as a nation.

—Mikah Griffin, age 17
(as cited in Howe & Strauss, 2000, p. 3)

They are in our classrooms as students, finishing student teaching at the university, and beginning to apply for classroom jobs all across the nation. They are well educated and open minded, and they love to collaborate. They are entering the schoolhouse with huge expectations, and if they are not pleased, they're only a click away from letting hundreds of friends know about it. When asked by the late Peter Jennings what they wanted to be called, they echoed in unison, "Millennials!" (Howe & Strauss, 2000). So Millennials it is, and we had all better prepare for their continued emergence, both as current students and soon-to-be teachers.

Born between 1980 and 2000, their sheer numbers rival the Baby Boomers. They are full of ambition, spunk, and confidence. In the book *Millennials Rising*, authors Neil Howe and William Strauss (2000) describe them as the "Babies on Board" of the early Reagan years, the "Have You Hugged Your Child Today" sixth graders of the early Clinton years, and the teens of Columbine.

As with other generations, Millennials have been shaped by the experiences and influences surrounding them while growing up, which included heavy doses of digital media. While Grandma and Grandpa hung out at the corner drugstore and Mom and Dad trekked to the mall, the sanctuaries of choice for Millennials are Internet cafés and cyberspace. My, how times have changed!

GENERATIONAL RECYCLING

Juxtaposed against the protesters who ushered in the 1970s and the home-alone Generation X of the 1980s, today's youth are shrouded in patriotism and protection. By some stroke of cosmic luck, surfer dude Jeff Spicoli from *Fast Times at Ridgemont High* managed to graduate and produce the smart, lovable Lizzie McGuire now attending Hillridge Junior High. Surely, Spicoli's teacher Mr. Hand would be thrilled to have the likes of Lizzie sitting in his classroom today.

How does it happen that the virtues of children can be so different from the virtues of their parents when they were children? It's really quite simple. Generational transformations are a cyclic event. Every 80 to 100 years, generations repeat themselves. In nonlinear, democratic societies such as America, this recycling occurs primarily for three reasons. According to Howe and Strauss (2000), each generation is

1. forced to solve problems that manifested during the previous generation's youth;
2. compelled to correct the behavioral excesses it sees in the current midlife generation; and
3. expected to fill the social role vacated by the departing elder generation.

In examining the parallels between Veterans and Millennials, consider how Veterans mobilized after World War II to rebuild the nation's economy, infrastructure, and civic pride. They relied on their collective power to change the injustices under which they had silently suffered— the Depression, feudalistic workplaces, a complacent government, McCarthyism.

Following the debauched, dispirited "Lost Generation," Veterans attacked every problem they encountered with cheerfulness, collective muscle, and a national conscience (Strauss & Howe, 1991). It wasn't about changing the system; it was about working within it. Veterans conformed, banded together, and showed up for things. Millennials seem to be slipping into the shoes of Veterans quite comfortably.

In *Connecting Generations: The Sourcebook for a New Workplace*, Claire Raines identifies eight major trends over the last 15 to 20 years that have shaped the personalities of Millennials. These trends impact how students and the youngest crop of teachers see the world, what they expect of themselves and others, and what values they bring into the classroom. Let's take a closer look at how these new kids on the block have been recycled (Raines, 2003):

1. **Focus on children and family.** The spotlight returned to kids and family in the years before and immediately after the millennium. With childhood sinking to the bottom of America's priorities during the 1980s, the pendulum swung back with destinations such as Las Vegas being marketed as vacations for the entire family. Parents and grandparents took children along to places across the globe. And eating out, once reserved as an evening for adults, became a family affair.

2. **Scheduled, structured lives.** Soccer camp, dance lessons, and tae kwon do have made this the busiest generation of all time. After parents, teachers, and coaches get done micromanaging their schedules, kids have little daylight left for free time or creative play. Elementary school students began using backpacks on wheels to manage their worldly possessions and Franklin Planners to keep track of their hectic lives.

3. **Multiculturalism.** Millennials have grown up with more daily interaction with other ethnicities and cultures than ever before. One in four comes from single-parent homes and three in four have working mothers (Goman, 2005). Friendships and dating have few racial or ethnic boundaries. Instead of guessing who's coming to dinner, parents are left guessing who isn't coming.

4. **Terrorism.** Millennials watched the bombing of the Federal Building in Oklahoma City. They learned of the tragedy at Columbine High School and saw school shootings become a regular news event. Of course, Millennials will always remember the catastrophic moment witnessed by the world on September 11, 2001, much as Boomers will remember where they were on November 22, 1963, when President John F. Kennedy was assassinated.

5. **Heroism.** As a direct result of these acts of violence, heroes reemerged out of the fabric of society. Policemen, firefighters, and even politicians were celebrated for their courage in times of great stress and danger. In the ten months following 9/11, the word *hero* found its way back into the American lexicon.

6. **Patriotism.** Disheartened by the post-Vietnam and Watergate eras, the patriotism of Boomers was sorely tested and much less evident than that of the Veterans. September 11 changed all that, too. Stores across the country sold out of United States flags within 24 hours of the collapse of the Twin Towers. While Millennials proudly don T-shirts with the stars and stripes, 30 years earlier their Boomer relatives participated in the public burning of the very same national symbol.

7. **Parent advocacy.** Millennials are being raised by highly involved parents who don't hesitate to intercede on their child's behalf. Parents argue over grades, engage in heated conversations with coaches over playing time, take their children on extended trips to visit college campuses years in advance of matriculation, and even traipse along to job interviews.

8. **Globalism.** With the advent of the Internet, Millennials feel connected to the entire world and communicate seamlessly with counterparts from Chicago to Calcutta. Globalization, according to *The World Is Flat* author Thomas Friedman (2005), is shrinking the planet from a small size to tiny. The power of Millennials to collaborate and compete globally is simply astounding.

The values developed in our youth serve as the foundation for what we believe as adults and how we raise our children. Think about how the argumentative, stand-up-for-my-rights Baby Boomers grew up in a time of postwar complacency. During their psychedelic rebellion, Baby Boomers took drugs to think outside the box. Now they pump their kids with Ritalin so they'll stay within the box. Or what about "Generation Wrecked," said to have been raised by wolves, who now refuse to let their own pups out of their sight? The generational lineup is constantly evolving and moving up a notch in the life cycle.

BYE-BYE, BREAKFAST CLUB

While it is difficult to make sweeping generalizations about an entire age group, and not all Millennials fit the mold, there are core characteristics that capture the motivation and academic values of Millennials. In fact, today's students (and tomorrow's teachers) have distinguished themselves from those of earlier times through several common traits. The desks of the downtrodden, delinquent *Breakfast Club* are now the desks of the whiz kids who leave adults *Spellbound*. If teachers continue to educate

Millennials the same way they educated their parents, the entire nation will be disappointed with the results.

To determine which strategies are likely to have the greatest effect on America's students, it is important to study their hard wiring (see Table 6.1, "Millennial Hard Wiring at a Glance"). Each trait has implications for how schools operate and how the educational community responds to student needs.

A SPECIAL LOT

Unlike their predecessors from Generation X, Millennials believe they are special and so do their parents. Schools are being asked to explain precisely how they will meet the needs of Johnny, since we all know Johnny is a "trophy child" who already knows an awful lot.

Table 6.1   Millennial Hard Wiring at a Glance

Special:	Older generations have created the sense in Millennials that they are vitally important to their parents, community, and the nation.
Sheltered:	Spurred on by the tampering with Tylenol, Amber alerts, and highly publicized school shootings, Millennials are the recipients of the most sweeping youth protection movement in American history.
Optimistic:	Full of trust, optimism, and an emotional connectedness to their parents and society at large, Millennials see the future as full of potential and theirs for the taking.
Team oriented:	Cooperative learning, copious team sports, and the media make this the most naturally collaborative generation to date. The Millennial code word is TEAM—Together Everyone Achieves More.
Conventional:	Proud of their own behavior and accepting of adult values, Millennials embrace the rules and conventions of society without much question or rebellion. Grunge is out and Abercrombie and Fitch is in.
Pressured:	Millennials accept the fact that they must study hard, compete for grades, and take full advantage of the opportunities parents provide. They've grown up with Mom and Dad proudly displaying "My Child Is an Honor Student" bumper stickers on the family SUV.
Achieving:	This generation has been bombarded with school accountability and the push for higher standards. Millennials may well become America's best educated generation.

SOURCE: From Howe, N., & Strauss, W. *Millennials Go to College: Strategies for a New Generation on Campus.* © 2003. Reprinted with permission by LifeCourse Associates.

As the charter and home school movements gain traction, public schools will need to market themselves not only to students, but to parents as well. After all, parents have invested so much emotionally and financially in their children's well-being, they cannot be expected to simply send them off to the neighborhood school without asking a lot of questions.

The first rule of thumb for educators is to get the parents of Millennials on your side. With them, you can do so much; without them, you may not make it around the block. Dealing with the high demands of both parents and students requires teachers to carefully monitor academic progress through frequent, formative assessments and introduce systematic interventions when learning lags behind. Moving away from large, end-of-course exams and grand projects spanning weeks to assessments that give ongoing feedback to the learner prevents students from slipping through the cracks.

Millennials and their parents fully accept the notion of No Child Left Behind and interpret it to be an entitlement to personalized and differentiated learning. Sweeping, comprehensive changes are what the school constituency has come to expect. Don't worry about overdoing it with this group because for many, whatever they are getting is not quite enough.

SAFETY FIRST!

Safety has taken on an importance like never before in the history of youth. From V-chips that control TV viewing, to contraptions that keep every object known to man out of a child's reach, to at-home drug and alcohol testing kits, worried parents have given rise to a number of profitable industries. As news stories such as the Polly Klaus abduction, the Columbine rampage, and the anthrax scare sweep the nation, parents demand heightened safety in schools as well. For sheltered Millennials, issues such as lead in the water, classroom mold, or dirty restrooms quickly take on a life of their own.

Rumors about such dangers move swiftly through a community and are told and retold from the baseball diamond to the floor of the pilates class. Alarms sound overnight on blogs and chat rooms in rural towns and urban centers. At one local high school in southern California's Capistrano Unified School District, comments on a blog a few years ago warned that someone was bringing a gun to school. Before administrators could react, over 50 percent of the student body had stayed home. Despite the best efforts of school officials and law enforcement, hysteria reigned as the remaining parents drove frantically to the campus to rescue their children from nothing more than a hoax.

Aside from dealing with parental frenzy, the district had to contend with thousands of dollars in lost attendance revenue resulting from the cyberalarm. For these reasons, Capistrano schools have adopted new technologies to communicate more expeditiously with parents. Listservs and prerecorded phone banks are used regularly to relay instant messages about safety. For example, after an attempted suicide in a restroom on the same Capistrano Unified campus, the principal got word out to 2,500 parents via e-mail and automated phone calls within minutes of the event. Parents were grateful for this advance communication. In responses back to the principal, many said that by the time their teenagers had made contact, they were able to provide the necessary reassurance and direct them to remain at school.

Administrators and teachers must assure parents and students through both words and deeds that they have their eye on every youngster. This doesn't mean policing Johnny's every move, but instead means sheltering him from anything that might cause physical or emotional harm. Designing schools within a school is one way that large campuses are making sure that each student is looked after. Smaller, more personalized learning communities allow teachers to keep tabs on their flock.

OOZING WITH OPTIMISM

Optimism oozes from the pores of Millennials. With the collapse of communism, medical breakthroughs continue to inch life expectancy upward and financial security is a given. What's not to be confident and hopeful about?

In a 1997 Public Agenda Survey, 90 percent of teens said they were personally happy and excited about their future (Farkas & Johnson, 1997). That same level of optimism applies as Millennials move into the workforce as teachers. Although they do feel stressed by their highly orchestrated lives, the percentage of college freshmen reporting "frequently feeling depressed" reached a record low of 7.8 percent in 2001 (see Table 6.2, "Happy and Hopeful"). Accordingly, youth suicide rates have fallen, not risen, as public opinion seems to indicate. For schools, this means an emphasis on positive outcomes and the replacement of realism with optimism. With Millennials, it's a matter of thinking win-win.

As confident and hopeful as Millennials are, they are also reluctant to stand out from their peers. A common Millennial credo is to follow the rules, work really hard, and don't mess up (Howe and Strauss, 2003). With a generation less comfortable working alone and very content with conformity, high school teachers may be frustrated by students' lack of

Table 6.2   Happy and Hopeful

Happy and Hopeful	Averages 1990–1996	Averages 2001
Percentage of freshmen who say they are "frequently overwhelmed"	23.5%	28.0%
Percentage of freshmen who say they will likely seek "personal counseling"	3.7%	6.6%
Percentage of freshmen who say they are "frequently depressed"	9.3%	7.8%
U.S. suicides per 100,000, ages 15–19	10.7%	8.7%
U.S. suicides per 100,000, ages 20–24	15.4%	12.8%

SOURCE: From Howe, N., & Strauss, W. *Millennials Go to College: Strategies for a New Generation on Campus.* © 2003. Reprinted with permission by LifeCourse Associates.

willingness to debate issues for which there seems to be consensus among their peers. Because taking risks is not part of this generation's repertoire, it may lead to classroom environments that are somewhat bland.

TEAMWORK: HERE, THERE, EVERYWHERE

Groups are the norm in the schooling and social milieu of Millennials. Students wear uniforms, learn in cooperative clusters, edit one another's papers, deliver team presentations, and get graded as one. At the same time, technology makes it a breeze for kids to stay in touch through cell phones, text messaging, the Internet, and Web communities such as MySpace. With serial ports, pairing, and personal area networks, Millennials synchronize multiple conversations with the skill and ease of an air traffic controller.

Command and control tactics don't bode well with children who want to be treated as valuable, contributing members of a team. As today's adolescents become tomorrow's teachers, they will expect to have the opportunity to work in groups, not in isolation, which fits in well with the ideals of the professional learning community movement.

> "We're seeing a huge cultural shift away from the word 'I' to the word 'We' in this new generation of young people coming in. And that's to be celebrated."
>
> —General James Jones, USMC Commandant (2002)

CONVENTIONAL WISDOM

The poster boy for the conventional Millennial is Harry Potter. Harry is portrayed in the movies as a bright-eyed young man in glasses, looking ever so traditional in his dress shirt and tie. He strives to excel in a very structured environment where students worry about grades and exams. Moreover, Harry and his classmates all belong to specific houses within the Hogwarts School: Gryffindor, Ravenclaw, Slytherin, and Hufflepuff, the model for collaborative teams. Contrast Harry to Baby Boomer bad boy, Danny Zuko of *Grease* fame, who cared little about what went on in the classroom or what teachers had to say.

While Boomers may have thought that no one was telling the truth in America, Millennials are more apt to accept the conventional wisdom of their parents, their teachers, or, as teachers, of their principal, than previous generations. In fact, they are more likely to impose some kind of order on the information they are given rather than to question it outright.

> "Perhaps reacting to what might be described as the excesses of their parents' generation, teens today are decidedly more traditional than their elders were, in both lifestyle and attitudes."
>
> —George Gallup, Jr. (2002)

In an April 2001 *Atlantic Monthly* article, columnist David Brooks quipped, "The young men and women of America's future elite work their laptops to the bone, rarely question authority, and happily accept their positions at the top of the heap as part of the natural order of life" (p. 40). All this means that principals must understand how to work with their new, young teachers. And how in turn to help them work with Baby Boomer and Generation X counterparts, who may find them to be robotic, mechanical, shallow, and a bit old-fashioned.

UNDER PRESSURE

Twenty-five years ago, the most worrisome issue in a teen's life was nuclear war. A decade ago, most teenagers agonized over AIDS and violent crime. Nowadays, Millennials worry most about earning good grades and getting accepted to college. In fact, being successful and soaring ahead are more important than ever, as social promotion becomes a thing of the past. As children spend more time on their studies, leisure activities continue to shrink or even disappear (see Figure 6.1, "More Work, Less Play").

Nervous parents rush to enroll their children in the rapidly expanding network of tutoring companies springing up in strip malls across America, including Sylvan, Kaplan's SCORE!, and Kumon. Summer is no longer a

Figure 6.1 More Work, Less Play

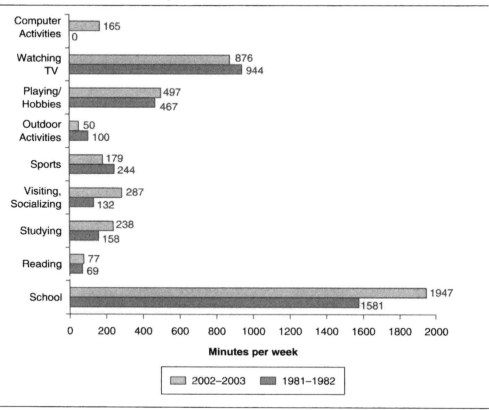

SOURCE: From Juster, O., & Staford, F. P., *Changing Times of American Youth,* © 2003. Reprinted with permission by Institute for Social Research, University of Michigan.

time to kick back and relax. Instead, Millennials enroll in boot camps with science and math themes. Coughing up big bucks to prepare tots for school, say many parents, is a small price to pay in order to give their children a competitive edge.

While some parents obsess over finding tutors, others camp out overnight to ensure their five-year-old gets into a good kindergarten. One California mother was riddled with guilt when she learned that despite arriving at 4:30 a.m. for registration, she was number 62 in line. "It's not as if this is a charter or magnet school," she moaned. "This is Long Beach, in a state that is 44th out of 50 in spending. . . . Is it too much to think your kid can get into a public school kindergarten without camping out as if you're after front row tickets for a U2 concert?" (Wride, 2005).

With all this added pressure, so, too, comes the likelihood of cheating. Two in five students say that half the peers they know cheat on tests (Horatio Alger Association, 2005). The prevalence of cheating has also been impacted by the convenience of technology. With search engines such as Google and Ask.com becoming ever so reliable, information that would have taken hours of library research to obtain is only a click away. Moreover, with a simple cut and paste and a bit of paraphrasing, Millennials can knock out a paper in a matter of minutes rather than days. Even *Cliffs' Notes* has been replaced by Web sites such as www.cheathouse .com, where entire term papers are obtained in a nanosecond.

To contend with these new developments, teachers are utilizing Web sites such as Turnitin.com, which scans student work for plagiarism and issues a specific report in a few short minutes. Driven by the intense pressure they feel, Millennials require the help of their teachers and principal to clarify values regarding academic integrity and the perils of cheating.

ACHIEVERS 'R' US

Millennials know that they represent a generation of high achievers, no matter what the newspapers might say about them. Media myths simply fuel the pressure they put on themselves not to fall behind the ever-present competition from among their own ranks. Unlike Vinnie Barbarino and his Boomer band of "sweathogs" or the Generation X pranksters always *Saved by the Bell*, Millennials accept high academic standards, large amounts of homework, and the intense pressure to succeed.

Contrary to what pundits would have us believe, American youth are achieving at rates like never before. Enrollment in Advanced Placement classes is at an all-time high. A growing number of students take the SAT to secure a passport to college. And SAT scores, along with graduation rates, are more promising than they have been in decades. As Table 6.3, "SAT Scores 1981–2002" illustrates, gains were noted across all ethnic groups when comparing SAT scores from 1981 to those from 2002. The gains were especially strong in mathematics.

Schools must react to this generation that takes technology for granted and views access to it as a must. Having been raised in a networked, mobile world, Millennials don't see gadgetry as high tech, but rather as rudimentary tools to do their work and be successful. Library stacks and microfiche readers are foreign to plugged-in

> "It was one of the few things a high school senior could depend on: Maintain a B+ average and waltz into a major public university. Not any more. These days, even a perfect 4.0 grade-point average doesn't guarantee admission."
>
> —Washington Post (2000)

Millennials. Online learning will become increasingly important as this generation enters the workplace as teachers, seeking continuing education

Table 6.3   SAT Scores 1981–2002

| | Verbal | | | | Math | | | | |
	1981	Original	Recentered	2002	Gain	1981	Original	Recentered	2002	Gain
White	519	442	519	527	8	509	483	509	533	24
Black	412	332	408	431	19	391	362	391	427	36
Asian	474	397	477	501	27	512	513	535	569	57
Mexican	438	373	452	446	8	447	415	447	457	10
Puerto Rican	437	361	440	455	18	428	396	428	483	20
American Indian	471	391	471	479	8	463	425	457	483	20

SOURCE: Copyright © 2006 The College Board. Reproduced with permission.

leading to column advancement and more degrees. In turn, Millennials may push the definition of schooling to make distance learning de rigueur.

WHEN THEORY MEETS PRACTICE

So how do school leaders translate all of this into practice with Millennial teachers on staff now and with those who will soon stream out of the university and into the classroom? What kind of environment will attract, retain, and motivate Millennial teachers? Is there a way to connect faculty from the Class of 2004 (see sidebar) with faculty from the Class of 1984 or 1974?

Class of 2004

Beloit College Professor Tom McBride has assembled a list of major ways in which Millennials have experienced life differently from other living age groups. Among the highlights from the Class of 2004 are the following:

1. The year they were born, Dustin Hoffman wore a dress and Julie Andrews a tuxedo.

2. Elton John is only heard on easy listening radio stations.

3. They feel more danger from having sex and being in school than from possible nuclear war.

4. They have never used a bottle of "white out."

5. If they vaguely remember the night the Berlin Wall fell, they are probably not sure why it was up in the first place.

6. Somebody named George Bush has been on every national ticket, except one, since they were born.

SOURCE: From Howe, N., & Strauss, W. *Millennials Go to College: Strategies for a New Generation on Campus*, © 2003. Reprinted with permission by LifeCourse Associates.

Strong school cultures will welcome Millennial staff with all the pomp and circumstance they can muster. With a high tolerance for change and innovation, a young teacher's biggest worry isn't being fired—it's being bored. Fostering collaborative learning communities where eager newcomers are seen as an asset, rather than a threat, is achieved through principled leadership and supervision (Raines, 2003).

• **Be their leader.** Having been raised under intense structure and supervision, Millennials want leaders who look out for their best interests. Bosses are expected to be honest and have integrity. It's not that they don't want to be leaders themselves; Millennials just want to learn from great role models first.

- **Challenge them.** This generation thrives on learning and wants to work on projects from which they can grow. They enjoy creating their own personal development plans and seek career paths that are loaded with opportunity.

- **Let them work with friends.** Millennials want to work with people they like and have a strong desire to establish friendships on the job that turn into friendships off the job. Schools that provide for the social aspects of work, as well as develop a team approach to learning, will find Millennials reluctant to leave them.

- **Make school fun.** Humor, a bit of silliness, and even a touch of irreverence will make your school more attractive to Millennials. Don't assume that joy and laughter will happen through osmosis. School leaders need to go out and find ways to create an ambience of fun.

- **Show them respect.** "Treat our ideas respectfully," they say, "even though we haven't been around a long time" (Raines, 2003, p. 178). Millennials are avid achievers who want to be recognized for their excellence and effort. Pay attention to their thoughts and contributions. And reward them accordingly.

- **Be flexible.** This busy generation isn't going to give up activities just because of a job. Young people want control of their time and seek meaning in their lives beyond work. A rigid schedule is a sure-fire way to lose Millennial teachers to another school district or occupation.

Now that you know how to manage your Millennial workforce, how will you ensure the young clientele sitting in the seats of the classroom stay with you, too? With these soaring expectations, is there a way to mesh teaching and learning to sustain the attention of this have-it-all generation?

First and foremost, the best schools are replacing facts and repetition with literacy and logic. Teachers use ongoing measures to inform instructional practice and single out individuals who need additional help. True disciples of a professional learning community wouldn't think of waiting until the end of the semester to find out that their students didn't grasp a concept. Conversely, they wouldn't dream of spending an entire semester teaching Millennials what they already know. "Assessment for learning" as opposed to "assessment of learning" is a trademark of a Millennial-conducive environment.

Next, successful schools are establishing cohesive teaching teams in every nook and cranny, not just in random pockets of the campus. The

Figure 6.2   Turning the Tide on Teaching and Learning

- Nintendo Effect
- Give 'Em Time to Think
- Double Takes and Do-Overs
- Happy Campers
- Reward Rather Than Punish
- Scaffold the Interventions
- Upward Bound

entire staff participates in the collection and examination of data to monitor its efforts. With a mother lode of information waiting to be mined, effective learning communities know how to tap the right vein. Subsequently, they are judged by their results, not by their activities.

Educational theory springs into practice through a shared belief that all students can do rigorous work even if they are behind in school. At the same time, students who are capable of forging ahead are permitted to do so. Advancing Millennial youth to the next level requires "Turning the Tide on Teaching and Learning" (see Figure 6.2). Infusing proven practices with focused action produces a no-fault guarantee of success for every student.

Nintendo Effect

It is not enough that assessment feedback is accurate and consistent. It must also be timely. How many students would play Nintendo if their scores came back days or weeks later? Like electronic game vendors, teachers need to make sure their students come back for more. To guarantee they do, feedback to Millennials must be specific, accurate, incremental, and timely.

Give 'Em Time to Think

When Veterans and Baby Boomers attended school, it was all about blurting out the right answer. But a teacher's job now is to develop students who can process, analyze, and verbalize complex information. Thus Millennials need more time to think. Even when an answer is wrong, the best teachers stick with students by extending wait time, cueing, showing confidence, and rephrasing questions.

Double Takes and Do-Overs

Standards have helped flatten the bell-shaped curve. With plenty of A's to go around, Millennials should be encouraged to redo assignments and retake tests to raise a grade. Requiring students to attend a tutorial before a retake or creating alternative makeup exams places an extra burden on teachers. However, the spirit of redos and retakes conveys the importance of objective achievement goals and ensures everyone is capable of meeting them.

Happy Campers

During the transitional grades from elementary to middle and middle to high school, students can get lost in the crowd. To address this problem, some schools are offering two-week boot camps that give youngsters the chance to interact with other newcomers and quickly become comfortable in unfamiliar surroundings. Rather than a one-day whirlwind tour, longer orientations foster a sense of safety, camaraderie, ownership, and belonging—all of which are highly valued by Millennials.

Reward Rather Than Punish

How many students toss their notebooks out the bus window on the last day of school? Unfortunately, learning is not pleasant for every child. Turning the tide requires teachers to reward, not punish; to inspire, not isolate. Fifty years ago, students left school knowing 75 percent of what they needed to know for the rest of their lives (Barth, 2005). Millennials will leave school knowing only 2 percent of what they'll need to know. Developing voracious, lifelong learners isn't just nice to do, it is absolutely essential. Teachers have to show students that learning brings its own rewards.

Scaffold the Interventions

By assembling a scaffold of interventions, every member of the faculty assumes responsibility for achievement, not just teachers in courses where kids are failing. Quality interventions include (a) interdisciplinary teams who examine student records every three weeks, (b) mentoring between older and younger peers, (c) parent-teacher-student contracts that strengthen stakeholder commitment, and (d) guided study periods that ensure students receive targeted instruction in concepts not yet mastered. Scaffolded interventions are supported by the belief that all students can indeed learn and the capacity to make this happen resides within the school.

Upward Bound

Integrating a college-ready curriculum with school-to-work applied learning allows teachers to meet the needs of outcast Jeff Spicoli and smart Lizzie McGuire on the same campus. Academies in areas such as culinary arts, health and medicine, automotive technology, and visual and performing arts are springing up everywhere. In Minneapolis, for example, low-income freshmen from four local high schools spent five weeks living in the dorms of the University of Minnesota sifting through clues to solve a mock murder (Resele, 2005). This CSI-inspired course places students in the role of police officer, coroner, reporter, forensic expert, and so forth. What better way to blend the study of anatomy, physiology, entomology, taxonomy, and physics all in one? Making sure Millennials are upward bound, whether they come from privileged backgrounds or are economically disadvantaged, is a great equalizer.

CONCLUSION: IN GOOD HANDS

While their grandparents found independence on the bicycle and their parents discovered freedom in their cars, Millennials are latching on to autonomy in cyberspace. As educators scratch their heads and wonder how to rein them in, kidlets scurry through the hallways IMing friends about the morning geometry exam and the evening Kelly Clarkson concert. At break, they Nextel their parents to confirm the limo will arrive by 3:00 p.m. to whisk them away to gymnastics before heading over to the Hollywood Bowl. With such full calendars, it is a wonder that Millennials even have time for school.

As with generations of the past, the hard wiring of Millennials poses a unique set of challenges for the adults responsible for educating them. Fortunately, the track record of teens marks a huge turnaround from the dysfunction and disengagement of Baby Boomers and Generation X. Contrary to what naysayers would have us believe, Millennials aren't antisocial, drug and sex crazed, prone to violence, or failing in school. In spite of recent events such as the shooting spree at a middle school in Red Lake, Minnesota, the tragedy in Tennessee after a student opened fire on the principal and two assistant principals, or skewed television features such as "Stupid in America," modern youth is not a mess.

Pessimistic views of Millennials are way off the mark as the nation's children soar from average to improved. Every youth indicator says our students are academically, socially, and emotionally better off than their parents (Howe, 2005):

- Rates of violent teen crime have dropped 70 percent during the last decade.
- Teen pregnancies are at the lowest level ever measured.
- High school sexual activity has dipped to 15 percent.

- Alcohol and tobacco use among 8th, 10th, and 12th graders has decreased significantly.
- Aptitude test scores have risen or at least flattened across all subject areas and all racial and ethnic groups since the late 1980s.
- Nearly two-thirds of middle and high school students say they do volunteer work after school and on weekends.

Can it be that the flaws and imperfections of their own teenage years have prompted Baby Boomer and Generation X parents to raise their off-spring better? If there ever were a generation that could "have it all," it might be the Millennials, especially if they can unplug themselves from their iPods long enough to connect with the rest of us.

Teachers and administrators need to harness the interests and capabilities of this remarkable age group. Forget lecturing Millennials about the information superhighway. They have been speeding down it since birth. Forget sweeping gay marriage under the rug. They have been living in same-sex households for years. Forget trying to put a spin on adult indiscretions. Millennials are quite familiar with the story of the president and the blue dress. And forget trying to pretend that problems such as homelessness, poverty, or greenhouse gases will fix themselves. Savvy tweens know better.

As the most socially conscious, community-oriented, and confident generation of modern times, America's future is in good hands. If we were the betting kind, our money would definitely be on the Millennials.

Meet the Parents

Rather than honing their own sense of direction, parents of teens of means have become a virtual GPS device that does it for them.

—William H. Caskey

After finishing a long day teaching her 33 kindergarten students, the teacher sinks exhaustedly into her chair. Seconds later the door is flung open and a distraught mother frantically cries out, "Where's Tyler's blue scarf?" Seeing the scarf around Tyler's neck, the teacher replies defensively, "He's wearing a blue scarf!" "It's the wrong scarf!" the mother exclaims. "Tyler's scarf is knit with yarn that exactly matches the color of his eyes!"

This story typifies some of the exchanges that occur between classroom teachers and the parents of Millennials. As discussed in the previous chapter, each generation of students brings its own history, strengths, and challenges to campus life. But, in the case of Millennials, they also bring along their parents, who act in ways never before imagined. With parents demanding more, questioning more, and around more, educators must rethink these vital partnerships.

In the not-too-distant past, schools dictated when campuses were open and when they were closed. Nowadays, parents appear at any time of day or evening, interrupting instruction to have a problem solved or barging into the principal's office to complain about their teenagers not getting a parking pass. Even Madonna—her "Papa Don't Preach" years long gone—is on a mission to save our children. She brags of taking a tough stance on homework, tidiness, and chores. Imagine the Queen of

MTV not letting her own kids watch TV. Listen to how a columnist from the *San Francisco Chronicle* summed up this cocoon of support:

> We MAPPIES (Middle-aged Professional Parents) have elevated child rearing to a sacrament. We arrange our schedules around our children's soccer games, volunteer as much as we can in the classroom, hover over every science project and book report, and take our kids on outings with such frequency that it makes our own parents snort and roll their eyes. (Zemke, Raines, & Filipczak, 2000, p. 130)

Regardless of how Mom and Dad are perceived, educators must recognize and empathize with the circumstances in which parents find themselves. Although parents may be experiencing a learning curve, so too are teachers and administrators. While it is the nature of Boomers and Generation X to micromanage their kids' lives and rescue them from adversity, it is the nature of educators to lecture parents about cutting the cord and letting children learn from their mistakes. The way teachers interfaced in the past with hands-off Veteran parents is not likely to work with hands-on Boomer and Generation X parents.

FLY-OVERS AND SWOOP-INS

Although there is no way to track the ages of parents with school children, it is estimated that the majority of high school parents are the driven-to-succeed Baby Boomers. With a history of getting their own way, these experienced moms and dads are devoted to making sure their offspring remain perfect specimens of themselves. Teachers recognize them as the pioneers of second, third, and fourth chances.

Sometimes referred to as "helicopter parents," Baby Boomers hover constantly, are ultraprotective, don't want to let go, and enlist a panel of experts—physician, lawyer, and counselor—to assert a variety of special needs and interests (Howe & Strauss, 2000, p. 71). The lives of these Renaissance kids are strategically planned—from the womb to college; from college to career; from career to marriage; from marriage to buying a new home (which is close to Mom and Dad, of course); and from the conception of the first grandchild to the delivery of the first grandchild. Without all the fluttering, the circle of life simply would not be complete.

The same Boomers who tried to distance themselves from their own parents have transferred this independence into control over the lives of their offspring. The irony is that Millennials don't seem to mind a bit and remain quite close to Mom and Dad. Even during the tumultuous teens, a recent

Figure 7.1 Family Ties

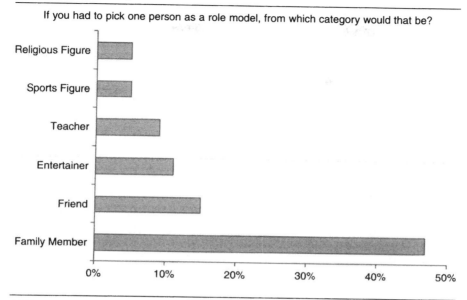

SOURCE: From Horatio Alger Association of Distinguished Americans, © (2005). *The state of our nation's youth.* Alexandria, VA: http//www.horatioalger.org/pubmat/surpro.cfm

study revealed that nine in ten high school students feel that they can confide in and talk to at least one family member at home (Horatio Alger Association, 2005). When asked to share the profession or social network from which students would select a role model, 47 percent said from their family (see Figure 7.1, "Family Ties"). Among these family mentors, mothers were the most popular choice (41%) and fathers came in second (25%).

Beyond being admired, helicopter parents are undoubtedly well intentioned. But many psychologists wonder if some parents are trying to create a really terrific persona of a child or a really terrific carbon copy of themselves. Since scheduling their first play date, picking out the perfect preschool, and shuttling their kids from one sports season to the next, it is hard for Boomers to let go.

Parents of today's elementary and middle school students have their feet planted firmly in the regime of Generation X. The give-it-to-me-now attitude that launched the Internet age parlays into an expectation for tailor-made information to track their child's every move. With an added distrust of authority and government, Generation X parents demand greater transparency and accountability in how schools operate.

While helicopter parents hover and drop in whenever necessary, Generation X parents are more like stealth bombers (Howe & Strauss, 2000). They move with stunning swiftness and are in and out before anyone even realizes they were there. Capable of penetrating thick defensive fields, stealth parents launch their all-altitude attacks in the grocery store, at church, or on the doorstep of your home.

Whether debating their child's grades, challenging the homework policy, or advocating for more time to prepare for talent show tryouts, Generation X got by without the system or anyone else advocating for them. As parents, they know how to get things done, how to get ahead, and how to use technology, irrespective of any rules or constraints the system may impose. Like the B-2 stealth bombers, which are thought to be the most survivable aircraft ever built, the Generation X parent machine can go on a long time without refueling.

When parents hover too much or launch attacks from a low-observation post, the consequences can be harmful. Teachers express concerns that students unable to do things independently may lack independence as adults. As Millennials meet the real world at some inevitable point, experts fear they may shatter.

Children accustomed to having everything done for them or who are constantly rescued from adversity, according to professor of pediatrics Dr. Mel Levine, are undermined later in life when they attempt to strike off on their own. Levine believes that years of parenting and schooling are missing the elusive mark of work-life readiness. Many high school graduates, he says, display the dubious trait of "well roundedness." But this very versatility makes it hard for them to commit to the narrow grooves of adult work life (Levine, 2005, p. 5).

Rather than blindly coping with adult overstimulation, educators are far better served trying to get on the same page with Mom and Dad. And when the teacher's suggestions are presented in a gentle, respectful manner, parents are more apt to accept professional advice. However, if a condescending or accusatory tone is used, these helicopters and stealth bombers will continue to fly over and swoop in whenever they see fit (Levine, 2005).

- **Easy does it.** Every time parents do something for their children, suggest that they do it slowly and make the child watch closely, so that the child learns how to do it on his or her own. This applies to tying a shoe, loading the dishwasher, or ironing a shirt.
- **Who am I?** Children have to discover their own identity. When adolescents reach age 11 or 12, parents should spend time talking about their emerging strengths and weaknesses. Adult and child can then work jointly on plans to address any shortcomings.
- **Hurry down.** Some parents are so worried about their child falling behind, not meeting the standards, or not getting into a good college, there is a natural inclination to want to rush in to do everything for

them. Explain that when students complete math homework, make a diorama, or write an essay on their own, it builds confidence and strengthens learning.

- **Durable work habits.** Teachers are responsible for teaching kids how to learn; mothers and fathers should be responsible for teaching them how to work. Talk to parents about assigning responsibility around the house and making sure homework deadlines are met. Teenagers should be encouraged to find part-time jobs. Adolescents need plenty of practice delaying gratification, staying organized, and developing a durable work temperament.

- **Don't make childhood an impossible act to follow.** Caution parents about overindulging children with spectacular vacations, opulent possessions, or relentless tides of afterschool and summer activities. Talk about how hyperinflated egos may actually burst in the early stages of a career when Boomer and Generation X bosses won't care a lick how pretty their daughter is or what a great ballplayer their son was in high school.

Teachers and principals can continue to bemoan how pushy parents have become, or they can step to the parent's side and try to understand the generational trademarks that are driving this behavior. When parents and educators meet in the schoolhouse, they each bring their own "auto-biographical scripts" to the table, which include memories of their school years (Lawrence-Lightfoot, 2003). These subconscious replays are powerful forces in defining the trajectory of parent-staff interaction.

Searching for common interests and common understanding gives staff a better feel for how to respond to and win over parents for the benefit of students. For example, one teacher describes her initial conference of the year as a "listening conference" (Harvard Family Research Project, 2003). The first question the teacher asks is, "What is your child good at? What does he or she enjoy?" Learning all she can about the talents the young person brings to the classroom enables the teacher to build upon strengths and interests and move the student in the right direction.

Another vehicle to get on the same page with parents is to use objective data when discussing academic or behavioral information about students. Descriptive, individualized accounts of progress via stories, portfolios, and student work give parents the impression a teacher really does know their child. During any conversation, it is imperative that staff members remain compassionate and hopeful so that parents leave with the impression that the adults at school really do care about their precious commodity. On the other hand, framing dialogue or opinions around the generational ethos from a teacher or administrator's own upbringing or school experiences can be a double-edged sword.

LOWER THE DRAWBRIDGE

In a now bygone era, schools were like fortresses, opened up once or twice a year for back-to-school night, open house, and graduation day. Other than these events, parents were seldom seen on campus unless their child was in trouble.

In many schools today, however, you can barely walk down the corridors without tripping over parents. Whether volunteering in the library, reading to struggling students, or barbequing hamburgers at the faculty appreciation luncheon, parents are everywhere.

While rural and urban schools struggle with underinvolvement, suburban and affluent schools are swarmed by an army of volunteers. Principals share stories of adults waiting in line to chaperone field trips, sending midnight e-mails to teachers to lobby for the coveted job of room mom, or signing up a year in advance to work in the classroom. Some teachers complain that parents have ulterior motives.

There is no doubt that Millennials are under the microscope as their parents hover and swoop to see how their cherubs are measuring up to the competition. And no longer are such practices witnessed at just the elementary level. Consider this motherly episode as a poignant illustration:

It was a beautiful morning last May when Richard Hawley, headmaster at University School in Cleveland, Ohio, saw the flock of mothers entering the building, eager and beaming. "I ask what brings them to our halls," he recalls. "They tell me that this is the last day the seniors will be eating lunch together at school and they have come to watch. To watch their boys eat lunch, I ask? Yes, they tell me emphatically."

At that moment, a group of lounging seniors spot their mothers coming their way. One of them approaches his mother, his hands forming an approximation of a crucifix. "No," he says firmly to his mother. "You can't do this. You've got to go home." As his mother draws near, he hisses in embarrassment, "Mother, you have no life!" His mother's smile broadens. "You are my life, dear" (Gibbs, 2005).

It doesn't end in high school anymore, either. The drawbridge is coming down on college campuses as well. University administrators say they are inundated with calls and visits from parents bent on checking up on their adult children or stepping in on their behalf whenever problems surface.

Parental interventions range from lobbying fraternities and sororities when students aren't accepted, to calling the housing office and getting roommates changed, to extreme cases such as one mother who made a 150-mile round-trip drive to Atlanta four to six days a week to visit her freshman daughter at Georgia Tech. When Mom wasn't there, she called or e-mailed her only child to remind her of homework deadlines, upcoming exams, or class registration. "She's not really good with time management because I'm her time manager," Mom told a reporter (Cox News Service, 2004).

The assistant vice president for campus life at Emory University said parents often get upset with college officials when they are denied access to grades or behavior records, despite federal privacy laws that protect students over age 18. To many Boomer parents, it seems logical that if they are paying for everything, they should be entitled to the details. And believe it or not, Millennials aren't bothered by the fact that their parents have decided to tag along to college with them. If educational institutions don't lower the drawbridge on their own, parents will simply scale the walls of the castle to make their way inside.

OUTWIT, OUTLAST, OUTPLAY

As former elementary principals, one of the most dreaded parental issues we had to endure involved the arduous task of classroom placements. Few things have greater potential of sending parents into a tailspin than getting a teacher whom they believe is not good enough for their child. While Ward and June Cleaver let the school decide where to place Wally and the Beav, contemporary parents want to dictate who will teach their fragile cargo and how this cargo will be chauffeured through the learning warehouse.

To successfully manage "Let Me Pick!" parents, principals must first determine what is behind a particular demand. Ducking inside the office after class lists are posted and awaiting the cover of darkness to make the great escape won't keep helicopter and stealth bomber parents from finding you. Consider what might be driving parental desires or angst as you match up teachers and students:

1. **Fear of the unknown.** Not knowing anything about a teacher or whether this individual is going to love their child as much as they do is worrisome to a Boomer or Generation X parent.

2. **Lack of power.** The more parents are told they don't have a say in something vitally important to them, the more pressure they will apply to be heard.

3. **The rumor mill.** Rumors and/or a lack of factual information create preconceived biases and mistrust. Didn't we learn this in the story of Viola Swamp?

4. **Emotional baggage.** Parents may have had a bad experience with a particular teacher when this individual worked with an older sibling. Or perhaps there was a negative encounter between the parent and teacher in the community. Emotional baggage impedes rational thinking.

5. **Your problem is not their problem.** In the past, parents like the Cleavers viewed schools in a broader social context. Today, parents want the best possible education for their own child and aren't particularly concerned about what happens to the child next door.

Principals should never take parent ultimatums personally or view demands as an affront to their administrative prowess. However, before quickly saying yes or dismissively saying no to a parent's request, think things through. The "Survival Guide" in Figure 7.2 is designed to help principals handle "Let Me Pick!" parents in a manner that leaves everyone feeling like a winner.

Figure 7.2 Survival Guide: How to Handle "Let Me Pick!" Parents

Outwit	Outlast	Outplay
✓ Allow parents to give input about the kind of learning environment they believe their child will benefit from, without naming a specific teacher. ✓ Post class lists or mail course schedules early. This gives time for displeased parents to voice their concerns, rather than swarming the office the first day of school. ✓ Use data in making changes that are in the best interest of the child before school begins. ✓ Don't ignore the fact that you're not only placing the child, you're placing the parent, too.	✓ Set a policy that parents must wait one to two weeks before any class changes will occur. ✓ Schedule a parent meeting and invite last year's teacher and this year's teacher to discuss concerns and iron out the issues. ✓ Monitor enrollment to determine how any class changes may affect class-size ratios, academic/social balances, teaching loads, etc. ✓ After two weeks, most students have bonded with the teacher and have made friends in the class. ✓ When students go home happy, requests are often rescinded.	✓ Even though a teacher may insist on keeping a student "to prove the parent wrong," some parents might never accept the teacher. ✓ Help the teacher understand that the parent will likely go out of his or her way to unearth shortcomings. ✓ Reduce teacher defensiveness by explaining if they are criticized in front of the child, their credibility is undermined—whether what's been said is true or not. ✓ If your gut tells you this parent-teacher match isn't going to work no matter what, make the change.

MIND YOUR MANNERS

The participation of parents in the education of their children is unquestionably important. Truckloads of research have been delivered to schools showing the correlation between parent involvement and student achievement. With home-school relationships holding so much weight, one would think that committed teachers and administrators would do all they could to increase parental involvement and enrich the lives of children even further.

But what is not significantly addressed in this research is how to deal with Baby Boomer and Generation X parents who are so rude or unreasonable that staff turn and run the other way whenever they see them coming (see box, "When Parents Behave Badly"). Obnoxious or hostile behavior directed at the professional staff is something Veteran and older Boomers rarely, if ever, faced.

When Parents Behave Badly

- An Iowa high school counselor receives a call from a parent protesting the C her child got on an assignment. "The parent argued every point in the essay," recalls the counselor, who soon realized why the mother was so upset about the grade. "It became apparent that she'd written [the paper]."

- When an elementary teacher in Tennessee started 31 years ago, she was able to make objective observations about students without parents going off. But now every morning, the teacher finds herself putting on kid gloves to delicately handle children and their parents. "[Students] feel good about themselves for no reason," says the teacher. "We've given them this cotton-candy sense of self with no basis in reality."

- An Orange County, California, principal receives a scathing letter from the mother of a second grader after speaking to the student about an alleged visit to an inappropriate Internet site. In the letter, which is copied to the superintendent and entire school board, the parent writes, "This letter is to tell you how terribly disturbed we are about your interrogation of our son, Michael. Your accusatory tone implied a host of things, all of which we vehemently disagree with. Michael remains confused and damaged by your inappropriate interaction and has lost two friends as a result of this incident. This grossly unfair treatment of our son causes us to distrust your judgment as an educator. You are NEVER to call Michael into your office again unless his father or I are present and you are NEVER to ask him not to tell us anything you say to him."

SOURCE: Adapted from Gibbs, 2005; Capistrano Unified School District, 2006.

In a 2004 Public Agenda report *Teaching Interrupted*, teachers said they are being driven out of the profession by a growing "culture of challenges and second guessing" (Public Agenda, May 2004). Between anxiety over potential lawsuits and the tyranny of students and parents who question the teacher's judgment, a majority of teachers revealed they went soft on discipline for fear of the absence of support from parents and administrators. Over half (55%) believe that when districts back down from assertive parents it leads to more discipline problems in schools.

What makes bad parent behavior especially hard to handle is that educators are trained to be kind, gentle, and forgiving. Sometimes the safest way to avoid confrontation is just to give in and hope through appeasement these parents will go away. Teachers have been known to inflate grades and ignore infractions such as cheating because students tell them, "My parents will sue." Principals quit their jobs or ask for a transfer because parents haunt them even in their dreams. The concern with yielding to a parent's every demand is that it reinforces bad behavior and can lead to an intolerable working environment.

In spite of this reality, there is a lack of teacher preparation in university courses in the area of family-school relations. Although teachers know they have to develop strong alliances with parents, the majority say there are no conceptual frameworks or practical tools that model how to value parent perspectives and engage families in productive partnerships. Many feel vulnerable to the potential wrath of parents.

One solution is to make the family-school relationship a central topic in teacher and administrator preparation programs. Harvard Professor of Education Sara Lawrence-Lightfoot envisions a course called "Teachers as Ethnographers" (Harvard Family Research Project, 2003). We suggest a parallel course for administrators called "School Leaders as Ethnographers." The curriculum could focus on the skills of listening, observing, and documenting. Candidates would also learn about the social ecology of education. The purpose of such training is for educators to understand how children and their families navigate through various domains of life, while identifying the role schools play in this broader social context.

Another potential solution to lessen tension and stress is to shelter school employees from verbal assaults and unwarranted hostility that forces them to take cover. Although sticks and stones may break our bones, name-calling, disrespect, and threats of being sued can hurt public schools, too. Tolerance and civility are virtues that appear to be slipping away as Baby Boomer and Generation X parents become more harried, impatient, and downright nasty.

When unbecoming adult behavior finds its way into the schoolhouse, it terrifies staff and is the worst kind of role-modeling imaginable for children. School leaders have an obligation to respond to open displays of anger or disrespect in a firm, decisive manner.

To maintain decorum within the sanctuaries of our schools, school boards might consider adopting a code of conduct (see sample "Civility Board Policy" in Resource E). A policy of this sort must define expectations for respectful disagreement and outline the consequences for people who cross the line.

Make it clear to employees that a civility policy is not intended to deprive parents of their freedom of expression nor discourage them from voicing concerns. Rather, a policy of this nature is designed to maintain a safe, harassment-free workplace for teachers and administrators while also establishing a respectful learning zone for students. Although most educators recognize they are public servants, no one should be made to feel like a doormat. Incivility and adult bullying have no place in our schools.

DIFFERENT WORLDS

Not every Baby Boomer or Generation X parent is able to buy a laptop for their third grader or purchase their 16-year-old a brand new car. While teachers see affluent, well-educated parents as more assertive in their relationship with the school, poor and minority parents are often reluctant, uncertain, and overwhelmed by an unwelcoming bureaucracy (Lawrence-Lightfoot, 2003). As teachers try to deflect overzealous parents, they must also seek ways to get underrepresented parents more involved.

Surely, better parenting will ultimately help underperforming students do better. But it is wrong for educators to say that good parents raise successful kids and bad parents raise dropouts and delinquents. In upper-middle-class homes, parents are able to invest time and money into making sure children have an array of learning experiences. Unfortunately, for many disadvantaged families, this simply is not possible.

In lower income and working-class homes, parents are more concerned about putting food on the table and taking care of adult needs. In this world, sociologists believe, there is a clear distinction between the child's priorities (school, homework, friends, play) and the adult's priorities (paying rent, doing laundry, going out, worrying about work). While wealthier families are recognized as being more child centered, lower socioeconomic families are typically more adult centered. The result is that children in these homes do not have as much attention paid to their academic or emotional needs. Subsequently, there is less parent involvement at school, lower expectations, and poorer achievement.

Be mindful of the fact that many minority and low-income parents do not view schools as caring places where the feelings and attitudes of children matter much. Despite the pleas from schools asking for their involvement, many of these parents are skeptical of staff's sincerity. This mistrust and suspicion is often viewed by teachers as indifference.

If education is to be the great equalizer, then it is the school's job to bridge the different student worlds. To even things out, teachers and administrators have to rethink the ritualized systems created by earlier generations that keep working-class families at bay—parent conferences scheduled between 8:00 a.m. and 3:00 p.m.; back-to-school nights where parents sit in straight rows listening to the teacher lecture about rules and expectations; PTA meetings riddled with innocuous topics such as who's in charge of water for the Jogathon; and booster club fundraisers where the country club elite auction off $5,000 parking spaces to send the football team to an exhibition game in Hawaii.

Traditional avenues educators have relied on to bring parents to school are more like "institutionalized ways of establishing boundaries between insiders (teachers) and interlopers (parents) under the guise of polite conversation" (Whitaker, 2001, p. 32). Sadly, these contrived events reaffirm idealized home-school partnerships, but seldom provide the opportunity for any meaningful level of interaction.

Although there may be disenfranchised or difficult parents who appear not to care about their child's education, diverse cultural and economic backgrounds create the need for schools to structure activities so that all parents can become engaged (see Figure 7.3, "Down-Home Involvement"). Not every Baby Boomer dad drives a Hummer or Generation X mom has the luxury of staying home.

As adults of all generations find themselves working longer hours and under greater stress, it is the school's job to show that spending 15 minutes here or 20 minutes there can reap big rewards for their children. Shorter, more frequent exchanges between parents and school staff are far better than once-a-year formal meetings where both parent and teacher feel the strain of being on stage.

Figure 7.3   Down-Home Involvement

Resources 'R' Us: Set up a room where parents can come and use the Internet, check out resources, or talk to other adults about parenting issues. This room should be run by empathetic, like-minded parents so that it feels welcoming to those who are not normally involved at school. The goal is to minimize any distinctions between the haves and have-nots.

Drive-Thru Coffee Bar: One of the best opportunities for principals to be visible and chitchat with parents is during morning drop-off. Once a week, with the help of the parent organization, principals can host a latte klatch as Mom and Dad breeze through the parking lot.

Wake Up to Books: Invite parents to drop in before school and lounge alongside their son or daughter to read. While Dad scours the *Auto Trader,* Billy can finish his chapter of *To Kill a Mockingbird.* Twenty minutes of quality time sitting in a classroom without anyone discussing deficiencies is a bonding experience. It also lowers the blood pressure of all parties—parent, teacher, and student.

Bearers of Good News: Educators are notorious for being the bearers of bad news. Yet, altering this reputation is easy if new routines are established. Calling the parents of one or two students each month to sing the youngster's praises is a worthy cause. Imagine the impact on Dad to receive happy news at work from a teacher. Or how about Mom listening to a warm greeting from the principal on the home answering machine and can't wait to replay the message for Grandma and Grandpa, too? Most Boomers and Generation X parents will tell you, "The only time my mom or dad ever heard from the school was when I was in trouble."

Dad's Club: An excellent way for fathers to pool their collective muscle and make nonacademic contributions to their child's education is through a dad's club. With all the fixing, installing, moving, and painting schools need, there is plenty of work to go around. Dad's club projects can coincide with events that link schoolwide goals. For example, the PTA may host a fundraiser for students to paint tiles for a Wall of Fame. Skilled dad's club members can build the display area and install the tiles. Dad's clubs are a fraternal venue for fathers to show off their talents without having to read, write, or do arithmetic.

Family Math Night: Events that draw an entire family—including older and younger siblings— are an enjoyable experience. Family Math Night is an evening of hands-on discovery activities where parents and children work side by side. Stations are set up around the school auditorium and revolve around engaging topics such as guesstimation, puzzles, and probabilities. Teachers act as facilitators while families wander in any order and at any pace. Parents and children find themselves in friendly competitions and debates around a subject worth talking about.

Preventive Maintenance: Don't wait until things disintegrate to talk to parents about a potential problem. And don't admonish or judge them when you do have to call with bad news. Making courtesy calls to explain why a youngster may come home upset, or to say there was an incident at school, lowers anxiety tremendously. It also builds trust between parents and staff.

DOES YOUR COMPLAINT POLICY MAKE THE GRADE?

Teachers are increasingly inundated with parental e-mail. It is not just the volume of e-mails that has teachers so concerned. It is also the expectation that each missive be met with an instant response. The "how is my kid doing" or "please make an exception for Susie" quips can fill a teacher's entire day. It also places faculty in a situation of having to use instructional time to respond to parents. How does the tenth-grade teacher/coach begin to reply to this Friday afternoon request from a parent?

Dear Ms. Jones,

Please excuse my daughter Ashley and her friend Chloe from school beginning Monday, April 8–12, as we will be extending our Spring Break to spend two weeks in the Bahamas. The girls will try to finish their English homework on the flight back from Miami, time and circumstances permitting. Also, please be certain that Ashley and Chloe are not penalized for missing cheer practice.

Sincerely,
Melinda Vandergate

In a best-case scenario, individual teachers do not respond to requests such as that—the *school* responds through well-developed and explicit policies that spell out predetermined, systematic responses when such appeals are made by parents.

Another result of the information explosion is that it gives working parents more flexibility to be active participants in the day-to-day education of their children. Although this can have a positive outcome, it can also put teachers on the defensive. Think about why. During America's manufacturing and corporate dominance, working parents were not permitted to leave their place of employment and show up at school unless their child was seriously hurt or in serious trouble.

But in today's wireless world, dads and moms can take the entire office with them if they need to head out for a few hours of school business. There is even federal legislation that grants public sector employees up to four hours of paid leave per year to attend parent-teacher conferences. The tipping point for older teachers and younger, more hands-on parents becomes obvious in the following exchange.

After a Veteran middle school teacher refuses to accept a late assignment, she is confronted in the parking lot by the student's father. The father is insistent that his son be given another chance to make up the work and raise his grade. The teacher proceeds to remind the parent about the importance of deadlines and personal responsibility. The irritated Boomer shouts, "I'm a taxpayer and pay your salary. This is unacceptable!" Abruptly, he jumps into his BMW and heads straight to the superintendent's office.

Older teachers have a hard time accepting or understanding this drastic social change and are most resistant to bending the rules or modifying procedures. To them, it's a matter of principle. Impatient Generation X teachers, with limited practice in the art of compromise or negotiation, may just blow off parents and ignore their requests altogether. Thin-skinned Millennials have few experiences in which to base decisions as teachers. Therefore, they are likely to cave in quickly because they cannot come up with alternatives, nor do they want the parent to go to the principal.

In today's climate of Nordstrom's customer service, indifference to the needs and desires of an intergenerational constituency is unacceptable. However, if a school district maintains a strong focus on its customers, does this mean that staff members have to concede to every demand? Administrators need latitude in balancing parental demands against teacher resistance. Too often, disagreements snowball into an avalanche that takes hours, days, or even weeks to dig out of simply because everyone gets overheated.

School districts that spend an inordinate amount of staff time fielding complaints might consider a policy that outlines step-by-step procedures for handling concerns (see Figure 7.4, "Step-by-Step Complaint Procedures").

The goal is to create a process for accepting constructive criticism, while shielding employees from excessive or frivolous demands that prevent them from doing their jobs. If your organization already has a complaint policy in place, take the time to review it and make sure it still makes the grade.

CONCLUSION: LET'S MAKE A DEAL

Forming alliances to decide what's in the best interest of students will help every generation become more reasonable. Teachers from the Veteran and Baby Boom era must learn to accept the fact that one's long-standing reputation is no longer a guarantee that parents will respect or accept one's judgment. New teachers from among Generation X and Millennial ranks should factor in parental management as a key component of their training. Acting like a deer in headlights at back-to-school night will not impress the crowd, nor will it engender confidence in your ability to nurture and care for students.

For Mom and Dad, childhood experiences with school were sometimes negative or even traumatic. Some parents can barely read or write and may not have graduated from high school. Others may have made it through the system, but struggled immensely. Feelings of

Figure 7.4 Step-by-Step Complaint Procedures

Level I (Informal)

➢ The complainant must first interact with the subject of the complaint. If the issue isn't resolved at the direct contact level, the complainant shall confer with the immediate supervisor. If still not resolved, the complainant may proceed to Level II.

Level II (Formal)

➢ The complainant submits his or her complaint on the designated form to the principal or department head. The supervisor provides a copy of the complaint to the employee and investigates all facts.
➢ The supervisor communicates his or her decision, either finding no cause to overrule the employee's action or cause to overrule the action.
➢ If the complainant is not satisfied, he or she may appeal the decision to the superintendent.

Level III

➢ Upon review, the superintendent or designee shall issue a judgment or, as an alternative, may forward the matter to the Complaint Review Panel for an advisory decision.
➢ The Complaint Review Panel (comprising a parent, district employee, and community representative) will conduct a hearing with the complainant and render an advisory decision to the superintendent.
➢ If the complainant is not satisfied with the superintendent's ruling, he or she may appeal to the board.

Level IV

➢ The complainant may request an appearance at a regularly scheduled board meeting. The board has the option to (a) take no action, thus upholding the earlier decision; (b) reverse staff's decision; or (c) modify the staff's decision.
➢ The decision of the Board of Trustees shall be final.

SOURCE: From "Civility and Complaint Board" in the *CUSD Board Policy Manual*. Reprinted with permission by Capistrano Unified School District, San Juan Capistrano, CA.

defensiveness and vulnerability can take both educators and parents by surprise.

There is no doubt that parents, teachers, and administrators share a common passion about the welfare of children. Wherever passions exist, so too does the chance for misunderstanding and conflict. While parents should try to lighten up a bit, be sensitive to the fact that the passion you see in parents is the same passion that has read stories, wiped noses, and taught their kids how to ride a bike. On balance, we should always be grateful for parents who care so much that they are prepared to swoop down upon the school, whether it be in their SUV, their helicopter, or their stealth bomber.

Contemporary parents and contemporary educators have more in common than some might like to believe. Both are adamant that their opinions and desires be heard. Both want children to grow up to be well-rounded, productive citizens. Both are devoted to learning and improvements so each successive generation has the chance for a better future than their own. As with any flourishing partnership, each side simply needs to do its part. For teachers and administrators, it's about alignment, not alienation. For parents, it's about reason, not self-righteousness. More deal making and less deal breaking will breed inter-generational harmony and understanding.

Resource A

Attracting
and Retaining
High-Quality Leaders

DISTRICT INVENTORY

Review each item and indicate the response that best reflects your district's current efforts to attract and retain high-quality school leaders:

Finding Quality Candidates	Exceptional	Adequate	Needs to Improve	Does Not Exist
The school board and superintendent provide leadership in developing a district recruitment plan.				
Practicing principals actively support site-based recruitment efforts.				
The Internet is used to accept applications and provide access to district information.				

(Continued)

District Inventory (Continued)

Finding Quality Candidates	Exceptional	Adequate	Needs to Improve	Does Not Exist
Getting Prospects Ready				
The district sponsors administrative preparation programs with local colleges.				
Entry-level leadership positions are available to prepare prospective candidates from within.				
Assistant principals are groomed to be learning leaders and have a broad range of assignments.				
Supporting New Principals				
There is a structured orientation to the assigned school for new principals.				
Beginning principals are familiarized with the district culture.				
Trained coaches and mentors are available to work with first- and second-year principals.				
Helping Principals Grow				
Staff development is designed to support instructional leadership and strengthen the knowledge base of principals.				
Training for experienced principals is differentiated and based on site and individual needs.				
Principals are guided in establishing measurable performance goals. Time is set aside throughout the year to reflect on these goals.				
Keeping Good Leaders With You				
Support staff is introduced to help redistribute some of the principal's workload.				

Finding Quality Candidates	Exceptional	Adequate	Needs to Improve	Does Not Exist
Socialization activities—including collegial problem solving, job-alike time, and celebrations—are provided for principals.				
The work of a principal is valued and recognized at all levels of the organization.				

Scoring:

Give yourself **2 points** for every "Exceptional" response and **1 point** for every "Adequate" response. Award no points for "Needs to Improve" or "Does Not Exist."

Interpretation

0–6 points	Little or no effort exists to attract and grow quality leaders inside your district.
7–12 points	Some effort is in place to secure and retain would-be principals.
13–18 points	The importance of leadership development and principal support is on the radar screen. Progress is noted in one or more areas of forecasting and mentoring future leaders.
19–24 points	Substantial gains have been made in inspiring and sustaining strong administrative candidates for leadership positions.
25–30 points	Congratulations! The district is doing a remarkable job finding, coaching, and keeping quality principals and coadministrators. Your organization serves as a model for others.

SOURCE: Lovely, S. (2004). *Staffing the Principalship*-Fig. 1.1 p. 16–17. Reprinted by Permission: The Association for Supervision and Curriculum Development is a worldwide community of educators advocating sound policies and sharing best practices to achieve the success of each learner. To learn more, visit ASCD at www.ascd.org

Resource B

Snag the Best and Bypass the Rest

Behavioral-Based Interview Questions

Background

Traditional interview questions often used to hire teachers can be leading and may communicate the answers an interviewee thinks the interviewer wants to hear. Rehearsed responses don't give principals insight into how a teacher might actually behave in a given situation.

Purpose

Assessing knowledge through questions about content and best practices is certainly important. However, the majority of queries should be structured to reveal the "intangibles"—those natural talents that absolutely must exist for a teacher to be effective. The secret to snagging the best and bypassing the rest is to hire for fit and train for skill.

Sample Questions

- Describe a time that you used persuasion to convince someone to see things your way.
- Talk about a stressful teaching (or work) experience that demonstrates your coping skills.

- Tell us about a time when you used good judgment or logic to solve a problem.
- Share an example of how your communication skills have influenced a parent's or colleague's opinion.
- Describe a situation where you had to conform to a policy/procedure you didn't agree with.
- Discuss an important project you've completed recently. Why was this project so significant?
- Share what you have done (or how you feel) when a student isn't learning.
- Explain how you prioritize instructional tasks when there is so much content to cover in a school year.
- Tell us about a time when a parent didn't agree with your homework (or grading) policy.
- Provide an example of how you have successfully dealt with another person even though that individual did not like you (or vice versa).
- Describe a team project you have participated in where a colleague disagreed with your ideas. What did you do?
- Tell us about an encounter you've had with a coworker who was not completing his or her share of the work. Whom, if anyone, did you talk to about it?
- Describe the kind of principal who has created the most beneficial working/learning environment for you.
- Provide an example of a difficult decision you were forced to make recently.
- Tell us about a book you have read recently on X. Explain how you used an idea from this book to impact student learning.

Resource C

Partnership Teaching Contract Language

1.0. Partnership Teaching Assignment
Generally, this program will be available to teachers assigned to elementary grades only. The feasibility of the program will be reviewed on an annual basis.

1.1. All teachers participating in partnership assignments must have permanent status and have a history of satisfactory or above-average performance.

1.2. Approval of a partnership teaching contract shall include, but not be limited to, the following criteria:
   1.2.1. Partners' compatibility. For example, teaching styles, educational philosophy, and work ethic.
   1.2.2. Commitment to and compatibility with the school's educational philosophy and goals.
   1.2.3. Ability to provide coverage for one another.

1.3. Partnerships shall conform to one of the following models:
   1.3.1. Two teachers sharing one classroom—dividing the workweek into three days and two days. By agreement, teachers may switch their assignments at the semester.
   1.3.2. Two teachers sharing one classroom dividing the workweek, with each teacher assigned two days and the fifth day, alternating on a regular schedule.

1.3.3. The final decision on the model to be adopted will be made by the principal with input from the affected teachers.

1.4. Both partners will participate in Back-To-School Night, Open House, first/last student days, preservice days, and parent conferences. During parent conferences, parents shall have the opportunity to meet with both teachers on specified days.

1.5. A total plan for the year must be outlined on the district form by the teachers requesting the partnership. This plan will include the following:

1.5.1. The specific dates each teacher is scheduled to work.

1.5.2. An instructional planning and communication system.

1.5.3. A description of how all adjunct duties will be covered and performed.

1.5.4. A description of how responsibilities will be met for covering parent conferences, staff meetings, and grade-level articulation.

1.6. In unique situations, the principal may require the presence of both team members.

1.7. Any teachers working 50 percent or more in a partnership assignment will receive district fringe benefits on a prorated basis. Teachers working less than 50 percent will not receive fringe benefits. Sick leave credit will be earned in proportion to time worked.

1.8. Partnership team members are expected to cover for each other in the event of an unanticipated absence. Substitute teachers will be requested by a team member only in extraordinary circumstances when such mutual coverage is not possible. Further, it is the team member's responsibility to obtain approval from the principal for such substitute coverage. If circumstances require a partner to be out more than five consecutive days, the extended leave provisions shall apply.

1.8.1. In the event that one of the partners must take an extended leave of absence but plans to return within the semester, the other partner is required to substitute at his or her per diem rate. If the leave extends beyond one semester, the partnership shall be dissolved, pursuant to 1.10.3.

1.9. Partners will receive credit annually for a full year's advance-ment on the salary schedule when a team member is on duty for at least 75 percent of the total number of student attendance days. Partners who do not work 75 percent of the total number of student attendance days shall be granted one year's salary advancement if the team member is on duty for 40 percent of any two years.

1.10. All partnership proposals shall be submitted in accordance with the following schedule:

   1.10.1. Partnership teaching proposals for the upcoming school year (including new and returning teams) must be submitted to the principal no later than March 1. The principal shall inform team members whether or not their partnership is approved no later than April 1. A team member may not withdraw from an approved partnership except for extreme extenuating circumstances.

   1.10.2. In the event a partnership assignment is not renewed or the partners or the district decide to terminate the partnership prior to or during the school year, the employee with the greater seniority in the district is entitled to the same position which the partners currently hold. In the event that the teacher with the greatest district seniority chooses not to retain that position, the remaining partner is entitled to the position. In the event that both partners have equal seniority, the surplus provision in the contract will be implemented affecting only the two partners.

   1.10.3. In the event that the partners terminate the partnership after accepting the offer as outlined herein and only one of the partners is able to continue teaching, this partnership will be dissolved. The remaining teacher will not be considered for another partnership until the next application cycle.

1.11. The principal reserves the right not to renew any partnership assignment if the objectives of the program or the criteria outlined are not being met and/ or will not be fulfilled or the instructional needs of the district are such that the partnership assignment cannot be allowed. If a partnership assignment is not renewed, the principal must notify the partners by April 1.

1.12. A maximum of two partnership teams per school may be approved each year. A principal has the discretion to add one additional team.

SOURCE: Adapted from the Collective Bargaining Agreement between the Capistrano Unified Education Association (CUEA) and the Capistrano Unified School District (CUSD). Reprinted with permission.

Resource D

Synergy Audit

How Generationally Friendly Is Your Workplace?

Directions: Read each statement and mark the number that most accurately reflects your current work culture. Be candid in your responses.	1 Never	2 Once in a while	3 Usually	4 Always
Seize Your Assets				
Staff members are viewed as important and trustworthy.				
Policies and rules positively reflect the value placed on people.				
The work environment is focused on the students being served and the strengths of the employees who serve them.				
Yield to Diversity				
The best people are hired—even if they look, act, and think differently from the rest of the group.				
Employees openly discuss opposing points of view and opinions on important issues.				
Communication is candid and honest, while respectful of cross-age differences.				
Nurture Retention				
Work assignments and adjunct duties are closely matched with generational preferences.				

(Continued)

Synergy Audit (Continued)

Directions: Read each statement and mark the number that most accurately reflects your current work culture. Be candid in your responses.	1 Never	2 Once in a while	3 Usually	4 Always
The school/district is concerned about holding on to the people it has.				
Building leaders look for ways to market the organization as a magnet for excellence.				
Exercise Flexibility				
Flexible work assignments are available to employees.				
People with flexible schedules do not encounter resentment from peers nor are they thought to be doing less work.				
Recognize and Reward				
Rewards and recognition are meaningful to every age group.				
The workplace embraces the mantra, "Do unto others, keeping their generational preference in mind."				
The school/district atmosphere supports playfulness and fun.				
Galvanize Learning				
A menu of professional development options is offered to ensure the continuous growth of all employees.				
Mentoring opportunities are available for new staff.				
Training is tailored to meet the unique needs and learning style of each generation.				
Yin-and-Yang Leadership				
Multiple perspectives are heard before key decisions are made.				
Supervisors are able to make exceptions without causing an employee revolt.				
Site-/district-level leaders support instructional alignment by linking ideas with the past, present, and future.				
Total: Add Each Column Going Down				

SCORING:

Add your scores from each column for a grand total.

INTERPRETATION:

70 or more: *Generational Landmark:* Congratulations! Your organization is managed to value and appreciate an intergenerational workforce. The atmosphere is collegial, is energetic, and supports high-performance teams.

60–69 *Synergy Rising:* Demographic time clocks are synchronized in several arenas. The pulse of the workplace is generally upbeat, with steady momentum toward raising employee engagement.

50–59 *Getting By:* Your school/district is typical of most others around the country. Although some good things are happening, more needs to be done to prepare for the cross-age diversity knocking at the door. Raise the happiness meter by applying strategies outlined in the synergy doctrine.

40–49 *Going Sideways:* Little sensitivity is shown for generational preferences or individual perceptions. Age-induced grudges often fester, which contributes to employee isolation, free agency, and/or dissension.

Under 40 *In the Gulch!* Your workplace likely suffers from higher than normal employee turnover and struggles to compete with the school/district next door. Staff members are working far below their potential and don't necessarily take responsibility for making improvements. Grab a shovel and start digging your way out of the demographic gulch.

Resource E

Civility Board Policy

CIVILITY POLICY   BP 1313(A)

Members of CUSD staff will treat parents and other members of the public with respect and expect the same in return. The District is committed to maintaining orderly educational and administrative processes in keeping schools and administrative offices free from disruptions and preventing unauthorized persons from entering school/District premises.

This policy promotes mutual respect, civility and orderly conduct among District employees, parents and the public. This policy is not intended to deprive any person of his/her right to freedom of expression, but only to maintain, to the extent possible and reasonable, a safe, harassment-free workplace for our students and staff. In the interest of presenting employees as positive role models to the children of this District, as well as the community, CUSD encourages positive communication, and discourages volatile, hostile or aggressive actions. The District seeks public cooperation with this endeavor.

Disruptions

1. Any individual who disrupts or threatens to disrupt school/office operations; threatens the health and safety of students or staff; willfully causes property damage; uses loud and/or offensive language which could provoke a violent reaction; or who has otherwise established a continued pattern of unauthorized entry on school District property, will be directed to leave promptly by the Chief Administrative Officer or designee.

2. If any member of the public uses obscenities or speaks in a demanding, loud, insulting and/or demeaning manner, the administrator or employee to whom the remarks are directed will calmly and politely admonish the speaker to communicate civilly. If corrective action is not taken by the abusing party, the employee will verbally notify the abusing party that the meeting, conference or telephone conversation is terminated and, if the meeting or conference is on District premises, the offending person will be directed to leave promptly.

When an individual is directed to leave under the circumstances outlined above, the Chief Administrative Officer or designee shall inform the person that he/she will be guilty of a misdemeanor in accordance with California Education Code 44811 and Penal Codes 415.5 and 626.7, if he/she reenters any District facility within 30 days after being directed to leave, or within 7 days if the person is a parent/guardian of a student attending that school. If an individual refuses to leave upon request or returns before the applicable period of time, the Chief Administrative Officer or designee may notify law enforcement officials. An Incident Report (copy attached) should be completed for the situations as set forth in paragraphs 1 and 2.

3. If any individual abuses the privilege of communicating via e-mail, that privilege may be revoked by the Chief Administrative Officer. Abuses are enumerated in paragraphs 1 and 2, but also include inappropriate use of the "copy to:" feature, excessive size or frequency of e-mail.

4. In the event the Chief Administrative Officer concludes that an individual has abused the privilege of communicating via e-mail, he/she will inform the abusing party in writing that all future communication will take place in writing transmitted via the US Postal Service. As an alternative or in addition, the Chief Administrative Officer may, at his/her discretion, arrange face to face meetings to discuss the party's concerns or a pupil's educational program.

Safety and Security

5. The Superintendent or designee will ensure that a safety and/or crisis intervention program is provided in order to raise awareness on how to deal with these situations if and when they occur.

6. When violence is directed against an employee, or theft against property, employees shall promptly report the occurrence to their principal or supervisor and complete an Incident Report. Employees and supervisors should complete an Incident Report and inform law enforcement about any attack, assault or threat made against them on school/District premises or at work related activities.

7. An employee, whose person or property is injured or damaged by willful misconduct of a student, may ask the District to pursue legal action against the student or the student's parent/guardian.

Documentation

8. When it is determined by staff that a member of the public is in the process of violating the provisions of this policy, an effort shall be made by staff to provide a written copy of this policy, including applicable code provisions, at the time of occurrence. The employee will immediately notify his/her supervisor and provide a written report of the incident on the prescribed form.

POLICY CAPISTRANO UNIFIED SCHOOL DISTRICT

Adopted: March 30, 1998   San Juan Capistrano, California

Revised: July 26, 2005

INCIDENT REPORT

Name: _____ Site: _____

Today's Date: _____

Date and time (approximate) of Incident: _____

Location of Incident (office, classroom, hallway, etc.):

_____

Name of person you are reporting (if known): _____

Is this person a parent/guardian or relative to a
student at CUSD?   Yes _____   No _____

Did you feel your well being/safety was threatened? Yes _____   No _____

Were there any witnesses to this incident?   Yes ____   No ____

Name(s) of witness(es): _____

Were the police contacted?   Yes ____   No ____

Below, please describe what happened:

_____

_____

If you need additional space, please use the back of this sheet. Thank you.

_____

Signature of Person Completing Form

A copy of this Incident Report should be sent to the appropriate Cabinet Member.

SOURCE: From "Civility and Complaint Board Policies" that appeared in the *CUSD Board Policy Manual*. Reprinted with permission: Capistrano Unified School District, San Jan Capistrano, CA.

References

Ansoorian, A., Good, P., & Samuelson, D. (2003 May–June). Managing generational differences. *Leadership, 32*(5), 34–36.

Bamburg, J. (n.d.). Learning, learning organizations and leadership: Implications for the year 2050. Retrieved October 19, 2005, from http://www.new horizons.org/trans/bamburg.htm

Barth, R. (2005). Turning book burners into lifelong learners. In R. Dufour, R. Eaker, & R. Dufour (Eds.), *On common ground: The power of professional learning communities.* Bloomington, IN: National Educational Service.

Bowser, B. (2001, May 24). Principal shortage. *Online News Hour. Public Broadcasting System (PBS).* Retrieved July 2, 2005, from http://www.pbs .org/newshour/bb/education/jan-june01/principal_05–22.html

Bracey, G. (2003, April). April foolishness: The 20th anniversary of *A Nation At Risk. Phi Delta Kappan, 84*(8), 616–621.

Brooks, D. (2001, April). The organization kid. *Atlantic Monthly, 287*(4), v40, 648–654.

Bureau of Labor Statistics. (2001). *The evolution of compensation in a changing economy: Report on the American workforce.* Washington, DC: U.S. Department of Labor.

Bureau of Labor Statistics. (2004, June). *Tomorrow's jobs: Occupational outlook handbook, 2004–05 edition* (Bulletin 2540). Washington, DC: U.S. Department of Labor.

Bureau of Labor Statistics. (2004, September 21). *Employee tenure summary: Employee tenure in 2004: Current population survey.* Washington, DC: U.S. Department of Labor.

Bureau of Labor Statistics. (2004, Fall). *More education: Lower unemployment, higher pay: Occupational outlook quarterly.* Washington, DC: U.S. Department of Labor.

Capistrano Unified School District. (2001, April). Civility and Complaint Board policies. In *CUSD Board policy manual.* San Juan Capistrano, CA: Author.

Caskey, W. (2004, October). Teens of means and the dangers of privilege. *University Business.* Retrieved March 24, 2006, from http://www.university business.com/page.cfm?p=631

The College Board. (2006). *Table 6.2: SAT scores 1981–2002.* Retrieved July 30, 2006, from: www.collegeboard.com/sat/cbsenior/equiv/rt021021.html

Collins, J. (2001). *Good to great.* New York: HarperCollins.

Cox News Service. (2004, November 23). *Parents of millennials tag along to college.* Retrieved March 30, 2006, from http://www.azcentral.com/families/education/articles/1123millennials-ON.html

CSR Research Consortium (2002, June). *Evidence inconclusive that California's class size reduction program improves student achievement.* Retrieved April 22, 2005, from http//www.classize.org/press/index-02.htm

Deal, T., & Peterson, K. (1999). *Shaping school culture: The heart of leadership.* San Francisco: Jossey-Bass.

Drucker, P. (1993). *Post capitalist society.* New York: HarperBusiness.

Drucker, P. (1994, November). The age of social transformation. *Atlantic Monthly, 274*(5), 53–80.

DuFour, R., & Eaker, R. (1998). *Professional learning communities at work: Best practices for enhancing student achievement.* Bloomington, IN: National Educational Service.

DuFour, R., Eaker, R., & DuFour, B. (2005). *On common ground: The power of a professional learning community.* Bloomington, IN: National Educational Service.

Farkas, S., & Johnson, J. (1997, February 11). Getting by: What American teenagers really think about their school. *Public Agenda Survey.* Retrieved August 18, 2005, from http://www.publicagenda.org/

Farkas, S., Johnson, J., & Duffet, A. (2003, June). Stand by me: America's teachers—don't make us scapegoats. *Public Agenda Survey.* Retrieved August 18, 2005, from http://www.publicagenda.org/

Friedman, T. (2005). *The world is flat: A brief history of the twenty-first century.* New York: Farrar, Straus & Giroux.

Fry, B., Bottoms, G., & O'Neill, K. (2005). *The principal internship: How can we get it right?* Retrieved January 15, 2006, from http://www.sreb.org/

Fry, B., Bottoms, G., O'Neill, K., & Hill, D. (2003). *Good principals are the key to successful schools.* Retrieved July 6, 2005, from http://www.sreb.org/

Fry, B., Bottoms, G., O'Neill, K., & Jacobson, A. (2004). Progress being made in getting high quality leaders in every school. Retrieved July 6, 2005, from http://www.sreb.org/

Garmston, R., & Wellman, B. (1999). *The adaptive school: A sourcebook for developing collaborative groups.* Norwood, MA: Christopher-Gordon.

Geraci, J. (2005, September). Learning from youth marketers. *The School Administrator, 8*(62), 24–28.

Gibbs, N. (2005, February 21). Parents behaving badly. *Time Magazine, 165*(8), 40–48.

Goman, C. (2005, September). Ready or not, here they come! *Link & Learn.* Retrieved February 4, 2005, from http://www.lingageine.com/company/news_events/link_learn_enewsletter/archives.aspx

Gordon, G. (2004, March 4). *Teachers stick with great principals, great schools, part II.* Omaha, NE: Gallup Organization.

Gordon, G. (2005, February). One vision, many leaders: Developing effective collaboration. *Eisenhower National Clearinghouse, 13*(5). Retrieved December 9, 2005, from http://www.adaptiveschools.com/enc/encpage4.htm

Gordon, G. (2005, April 20). *Replacing a generation of school leaders.* Omaha, NE: Gallup Organization.

Harvard Family Research Project. (2003, Fall). Renewing teacher-parent relations: Q & A with Dr. Sara Lawrence-Lightfoot. *FINE Forum e-Newsletter, 7.*

http://www.gse.harvard.edu/hfrp/projects/fine/fineforum/forum7/questions.html

Hegarty, S., & Gilmer, K. (2002, March 25). Once mighty teacher union's influence on wane. *St. Petersburg Times, South Pinella Edition*, p. A1.

Hess, F. (2005, November). Reform at the table. *American School Board Journal, 192*(11), 32–35.

Horatio Alger Association of Distinguished Americans. (2005). *The state of our nation's youth.* Retrieved February 10, 2005, from http//www.horatioalger.org/pubmat/surpro.cfm

Howe, N. (2005, September). Harnessing the power of Millennials. *The School Administrator, 8*(62), 18–22.

Howe, N., & Strauss, W. (2000). *Millennials rising: The next great generation.* New York: Vintage Books.

Howe, N., & Strauss, W. (2003). *Millennials go to college: Strategies for a new generation on campus.* Great Falls, VA: LifeCourse Associates.

Institute for Educational Leadership. (2000, October). *Leadership for student learning: Reinventing the principalship.* Retrieved June 21, 2005, from http://www.iel.org/programs/21st/reports/principal.pdf

Juster, F. T., Ono, H., & Stafford, F. (2004, November). *Changing times of American youth.* Ann Arbor: Institute for Social Research, University of Michigan.

Lancaster, L., & Stillman, D. (2002). *When generations collide.* New York: HarperBusiness.

Lawrence-Lightfoot, S. (2003). *Essential conversations: What parents and teachers can learn from each other.* New York: Random House.

Levine, M. (2005). *Ready or not, here life comes.* New York: Simon & Schuster.

Longley, R. (2005, June). *College degree nearly doubles annual earnings.* Retrieved October 2, 2005, from http//usgovinfo.about.com/od/censusandstatistics/a/collegepays_p.htm

Lovely, S. (2004). *Staffing the principalship: Finding, coaching and mentoring school leaders.* Alexandria, VA: ASCD.

Lovely, S. (2006). *Setting leadership priorities. What's necessary, what's nice and what's got to go.* Thousand Oaks, CA: Corwin Press.

Martin, C., & Tulgan, B. (2002). *Managing the generation mix: From collision to collaboration.* Amerherst, MA: HRD Press.

National Center for Educational Statistics. (2003). *Digest of educational statistics and tables: Selected characteristics of public school teachers.* Washington, DC: U.S. Department of Education.

National Commission on Excellence in Elementary Teacher Preparation for Reading Instruction. (2003). *Prepared to make a difference.* Newark, DE: International Reading Association. (Executive Summary available from http://www.reading.org/downloads/resources/1061teacher_ed_com_summary.pdf)

Nelson, B. (2005). *1001 ways to reward employees,* 2nd ed. New York: Workman.

Nelson, B. (2003, Fall). *What do employees want? Employee recognition practices inventory.* San Diego, CA: Nelson & Associates.

Nelson, B., & Spitzer, D. R. (2002). *1001 rewards & recognition fieldbook.* New York: Workman.

Orozco, L., & Oliver, R. (2001, July 1). A lack of principals. *Los Angeles Times,* p. B17.

Ouchi, W. (2004, August). Tilting the balance. *The School Administrator, 6*(26), 18–22.

Patterson, M. (2005, May). Hazed! *Educational Leadership, 62*(8), 20–23.

Powell, C. (2004, May). Diplomacy, properly understood. *State Magazine, 479,* 2.

Public Agenda Survey (2004, May). *Teaching interrupted: Do discipline policies in today's public schools foster the common good?* Retrieved August 18, 2005, from www.publicagenda.org/

Raines, C. (1997). *Beyond generation X: A practical guide for managers.* Menlo Park, CA: Crisp Publications.

Raines, C. (2003). *Connecting generations: The sourcebook for a new workplace.* Menlo Park, CA: Crisp Publications.

Ramsey, R. (2006). *Lead, follow, or get out of the way* (2nd ed.). Thousand Oaks, CA: Corwin Press.

RAND Education. (2003). *Are schools facing a shortage of qualified administrators?* [Online research brief]. Retrieved May 7, 2005, from http://www.rand.org/pubs/research_briefs/RB8021/index1.html

Resele, A. (2005, July 7). High school students turn forensic expert in U of M upward bound class. *UMNews.* http://www.ur.umn.edu/FMPro?-db= releases&-lay=web&-format=umnnewsreleases/releasesdetail.html

Ross, H., & Traub, L. (2004). *Managing a multigenerational workforce.* Retrieved May 15, 2005, from http://www.thediversitytoolkit.com/

Rutherford, P. (2002). *Instruction for all students.* Alexandria, VA: Just ASK Publications.

Schlechty, P. (1997). *Inventing better schools: An action plan for educational reform.* San Francisco: Jossey-Bass.

Strauss, W. (2005, September). Talking about their generation. *The School Administrator, 8*(62), 10–14.

Strauss, W., & Howe, W. (1991). *Generations: The history of America's future, 1584 to 2069.* New York: William Morrow.

Toossi, M. (2004, February). *Labor force projections to 2012: The graying of the U.S. workforce: Monthly labor review.* Washington, DC: U.S. Bureau of Labor Statistics.

Tyler, R. (1986–1987, December–January). The five most significant curriculum events in the twentieth century. *Educational Leadership, 4*(44), 36–40.

U.S. Census Bureau. (2004). *General demographic characteristics. American community survey.* Washington, DC: Author.

Wendover, R., & Gargiulo, T. (2006). *On cloud nine: Weathering the challenge of many generations in the workplace.* New York: AMACOM.

Whitaker, T. (2001). *Dealing with difficult parents: And with parents in difficult situations.* West Larchmont, NY: Eye on Education.

Wride, N. (2005, September 4). A slacker mother's self-loathing. *Los Angeles Times,* p. M6.

Zemke, R., Raines, C., & Filipczak, B. (2000). *Generations at work.* New York: American Management Association.

Zolli, A. (2006, March). Demographics: The population hourglass [Electronic version]. *Fast Company, 103,* 56.

Index